THE BOOK BUSINESS

D1741592

With leering looks, bull-fac'd and freckl'd fair,
With two left legs, and Judas colour'd hair,
And frowzy pores that taint the ambient air.

John Dryden on his publisher Jacob Tonson

THE
BOOK
BUSINESS

John
Baker

5 ROYAL OPERA ARCADE
PALL MALL LONDON SW1

© 1971 JOHN BAKER

First published in 1971 by
JOHN BAKER (PUBLISHERS) LTD
5 Royal Opera Arcade
Pall Mall London SW1

ISBN 0 212 98388 1

Printed in Great Britain by
W & J MACKAY & CO LTD, CHATHAM

Contents

Preface

This book is no great shakes as a piece of research or management literature. I wanted to make a few remarks about the business in which I have earned my living and to provide a front-line account of the processes of publishing and bookselling. The reader will naturally turn to Sir Stanley Unwin's *Truth about Publishing* or to Philip Unwin's *The Business of Publishing* for a more academic insight into the business of being a successful publisher.

I hope that the reader will find my comments, after forty years in the Trade, interesting and providing a sense of commitment, and therefore of enjoyment. Some will say that they represent the accumulated prejudices of forty years, and I hope I will not be grudged that pleasure.

Publishers and booksellers are several kinds of person, and the least classifiable of men and women. The most avid merchandiser longs to publish significant books and the most distinguished publisher hungers after a little bit of merchandise. Fortunately one does not always exclude the other. Publishers must respond to changing technologies and to changing social values, and the Trade will be very different in twenty years' time. But I am pleased to notice that, despite the urgings of *The Economist*, that publishers must pull up their socks and get into business, both sides of the Trade obstinately remain a mixture of commerce and vocation.

I am hoping that my subjective approach will make some appeal to the fringe public interested in the inside of the book business and to young men and women anxious to be 'in books' if only because at its worst the Trade is fairly innocent and, at its best, important. When I was young we used to talk pompously about 'the fabric of Western Civilization'. I dedicate this book to all in the Trade who have contributed to that ideal.

The Communicators

The book trade is not a dying trade although it is the despair of *The Economist*. It goes wheeling on despite the fact that it produces its books much as did Caxton five hundred years ago, that it is staffed largely by amateur and missionary enthusiasts, and that it is half a business and half a vocation. This is its distinguishing and unique feature over a large area of its activities. Although it has, curiously, always been known as the Trade it has never been able to be wholly that; and it is a solemn thought that, up to forty years ago, it was the only medium through which most of our people got their education beyond the three R's.

You would naturally expect such a business to be various in its populations. On one hand you have the professionals, who are acute, since they are engaged in selling something which the public doesn't actually need, and in any case can borrow; on the other hand it is blessed or cursed by the amateur with only a love of books, which he indulges in at the expense of a relative and either goes to Carey Street or, if the purse is long, learns in due time.

It has also been remarked that in no occupation except the film business is it possible to lose money in a brief period. Sums of £20,000 to £25,000 have been lost with only slight effort in post-war years. If this appear to be derisive to readers of the *Financial Times*, publishers are proud to point out the example of Simpkin Marshall, the great wholesalers, who performed the feat of going into liquidation with a deficit of £200,000. That was good going twenty years ago. It is perhaps a comment on the trade's respect for tycoons and the difficulties of its own affairs that practically every publisher in London was seriously involved in this collapse, but accepted without protest an accusation of lack of co-operation.

The economic bane of the traditional book trade lies in the fact that the production and marketing of books from the manuscript stage is an intricate and detailed affair and, at the sales stage, there is hardly ever enough volume to justify the elaborate expenses involved. It is as if you were designing and producing a car with the prospect of selling only a few hundred models at the end. Jonathan Cape, looking at a heap of manuscripts, and no doubt thinking that a couple of years would be needed for the translation from one medium to another, sadly remarked, 'Publishing can be made to pay if you don't value your own time at all.'

But it is not my object, at this stage, to speak particularly of the economic consequences of being in the book trade, but to look at them in relation to the status of books in a society whose social habits are undergoing rapid change. When Wynkyn de Worde said that with his twenty-five soldiers of lead he would conquer the world he was guilty of optimism, and was duly corrected by the cynic who observed that if books could change the world it would have been changed long ago. It remains a fact, though, as I have already said, that up to four decades ago there was virtually no way of spreading ideas except through the written or printed word. It is certainly not an exaggeration to assert that the spread of high civilization has, for some five thousand years, been so dependent; and today the book still occupies a vital place in our Western culture, not to say Mao's Eastern culture.

Malcolm Muggeridge recently remarked in an address to the Society of Bookmen that it would be possible for a person to grow up in the future as an intelligent individual without being able to read. This is not too ridiculous an assertion. We should by now have done with the snobbery which assumes the shamefaced ownership of a television set. Here we are face-to-face with printing's most formidable rival. Television is often bad or, at best, innocuous; but it is often too good for the printed word; and far too cheap. In some subjects it is a serious competitor with the printed word for leisure time. Time is not without end, and such challenges must, in terms of hours stolen from reading, amount to astronomical figures. One of the virtues of the radio was that it allowed you to listen with one ear, and, so to speak, read with the other: the art of reading while viewing is more difficult to acquire. Television is moreover producing a generation of children to whom books are a necessity at school and an anachronism at home.

But perhaps the most subtle enemy of leisured reading is the change in the spirit of the times. The climate of my youth was one in which the Log Cabin to White House motive was dominant. We thought of books as the key to a full life, and we were angry not because we had no money but had no learning. We had a religious regard, like Jude the Obscure, for the dreaming spires. We had no radio, let alone television, and our greatest satisfaction was to read an 'improving' book. We thought that if enough people read good books the world would become good. We patronized the local library, where the word SILENCE was displayed and heeded, where the musty odour was as wine. We revered the name of Andrew Carnegie and we went without lunch to buy and read the English classics at a shilling or two a volume; and we respected authors as god-like creatures; we would go to lectures for the pure pleasure of looking at them.

Today such simple enthusiasms are hardly to be found. It is no longer suggested that an understanding of books is the basis of fulfilment and a quoter from books is considered to be showing off. We are moving, rapidly sliding, into a culture in which books are not the basis of a liberal, humane life but are working manuals, political tracts, or part of the entertainment syndrome. There is indeed, in some quarters, a contempt for book-learning, in a literary or scholarly sense, and the *Financial Times* commented sharply that 'Oxford has ten chairs of history and none of physics' (1965). In such an atmosphere Government follows the trend, with a declaration that our future depends on technology and technical colleges, casts frowning eyes on the grammar-school syllabus and deplores the fact that many students still persist in humanist studies. On the way the cost of posting books is doubled and trebled, 'printed matter' rates are ditched, vicious taxation is levied on libraries and learned societies, 'Books, etc' (in Lord Hill's definition) escape by the skin of their teeth from purchase tax, and the Third Programme is virtually abandoned.

Since the printed word is, in some quarters, depressing the dignity of life (in the United States it is reported, in the *Daily Telegraph* (1969), that 20 per cent of all book sales can be classified as pornographic or obscene), it must be admitted that people become publishers from various motives: some are in it for money; some because it's a living; some because it's in the family; some for glamour and headlines; some because they see the opportunity—in a world of lost opportunities—to help mankind. In such company the consistent equation of publishing with the production of works of a high cultural level is too much to be expected. But the Trade as a whole is elevated by a surprisingly high degree of enlightenment and benevolence. Everybody has heard of authors being rooked, of their selling copyrights for a mess of pottage, and that Barrabas was a publisher; but the good books subsidized by publishers are forgotten. It has always been a tradition on the responsible side of publishing that, confronted with important work, a publisher must say Yes. I have known many publishers to lose money for a book's sake, make bargains for a cause's sake with the shadowiest basis of commerce, and very few indeed to get tough or to remain tough for long. So that publishers and booksellers are a little surprised and pleased at the end of each year to find that they have made a profit and can go on enjoying themselves a little longer.

It has been argued that publishers are their own worst enemies. Geoffrey Faber, writing in the thirties, when publishers suffered financially as never since, and the Trade was saved by the outbreak of the Second World War, blamed publishers for <u>overproduction</u>. His firm has amply demonstrated that physicians cannot cure themselves, since Faber now ranks among the top ten producers and issues more than 200 books a year. It has been said that British publishing suffers from underconsumption rather than overproduction, and while it is true that the rate of new production has been exceeded by the rate of overall sale, 30,000 new books and new editions a year is certainly too many. Even deducting the *biblia-a-biblia*, the structure of the book trade groans under the enormous burden. Reviewers cannot find the space and bookshops, already bursting their walls, cannot house even the good books. Publishers themselves have hardly the time to do credit or justice to, even to read, each of their books. It is common talk among publishers' representatives that when they have a dozen new books a week to show, booksellers tend to ignore most of them; and they must also find time to do other work than seeing travellers. In today's distributive system it is common for important works to fall straight from the printing press into limbo. There is little to be done about such proliferation. No power on earth will stop Messrs J. or Messrs B. from issuing dozens of books each month, and their bad books, their easy, cheaper merchandise, will push out the good. At times the situation is quite out of hand. In one week, in a recent November, W. H. Smith & Son had 600 new books subscribed to them, and were expected to buy supplies of each book.

It goes against the grain to criticize publishers for overproduction; and perhaps the chief glory of British publishing is that it produces more books per head of population than that of any other nation. That a publisher can produce, e.g., *A History of the Russians in Ethiopia* (subtitled 'An Essay in Futility') or a book on *The Georgian Theatre in Wessex*, to instance two recent examples, adds variety to fecundity, and may provide support for the view that the virtue of a civilization is in ratio to its production of books on interesting but obscure subjects.

Since the end of the last war printers have been awarded fifteen increases in wages. Inflation has hit publishing with more severity than other trades; and the cost of producing a book has trebled since peace broke out in 1945. Since publishers feel that the public will find itself unable or unwilling to pay this increase, they have been obliged to cease publishing, at a profit at least, many serious books for smaller markets. It is an axiom among scholars that there is no investigation without publication, and learned societies and their publishers are now trying to find methods for producing books of the non-Caxton type; and lithography, aided by the typewriter, offers promise here.[1]

By one of the ironies of history culture flourishes when people don't. Thus it was possible in the thirties to produce cloth-bound books for sale at a shilling, and a Penguin for sixpence. It seems to a publisher that every time he asks for an estimate the price has risen by ten per cent.

If catering for minority tastes, both in terms of creative imagination and information, is the hallmark of civilization, then it must be said that the inflation of the cost of producing books beyond the public's ability to pay is an injury to the quality of British culture. The full impact of inflation has yet to be seen, but if you seek a clue take a walk round the London library. There you will find a history of Leighton Buzzard or Shepton Mallet or books on the topography of the Andover region or the water resources of West Wiltshire. This is civilization that has passed away, though, through one of those quirks of human ingenuity, this statement is becoming less true as I write. Thanks to lithography a small group of publishers has arisen who make it their business to reprint out-of-print books in the fields of geography, social history and

[1] 'The pay increases for the printing electricians, which were back-dated 12 months, brought their standard wage up to £33.19.6d for a 40 hour week in return for agreement to co-operate in improving productivity. They had been demanding a rise of more than £12 a week to bring their wages up to the level of grade two machine minders at the Watford plant.' *Financial Times*, 13.5.69.

communications: at very high prices, and one has to distinguish, or attempt to, between useful scholarship and
nostalgia, for which there is now a big market.

The post-war inflation has produced a whole series of
problems for the newer publishers. On grounds of financial
resource they cannot publish, nor booksellers stock, slow-
selling titles. The basis of much serious publishing is the
assumption that an edition of a scholarly book can be
disposed of in three years for a profit of between 10 and
15 per cent of turnover. In the light of this circumstance,
and remembering that many books do not sell out completely, or take longer to sell, there is not much basis for
borrowing or financial assistance. Large numbers of books
are being allowed to run out of print (and as many
remaindered) simply because the money will not stretch
out, and indeed the pace of inflation is such that any new
edition will sometimes cost more than the original printing. It is a fact that any new publisher working on these
lines, and starting today, will find that two-thirds of his
working capital is in his warehouse in the form of books at
the end of his first year and the whole of it in that place
in the second year. The high cost of money in reprinting,
the introduction of immediate rental charges for type and
stock and paper, has the implicit effect of turning publishers
and booksellers into men who are likely to consider a good
book as one that sells out immediately and a bad book one
that sells more slowly.

Despite these problems publishing output continues to
increase and is now at 30,000 new books and new editions
a year; and, taking the swings with the roundabouts, the
big publishers do not complain, and, in our next chapter,
we shall attempt to understand why. Nor does the traditional old-time publisher lose money. If he has survived

the first dozen difficult years, and has behaved sensibly in building a foundation of back-list books, has not joined the auction ring for his front list, has not called heavily on loans or debentures, he may find it not too hard to make a profit.

Let us agree that, in social terms, the printed word remains the unique, perfectly born, mode of communication. You can return to it; you can re-read large or small portions and arrive at a comprehensive understanding of the author's purpose. You can carry a book around and read it wherever and whenever you feel disposed. The very act of reading or studying is probably in itself more educative since it involves effort and participation. Books can still be addressed to small publics, unthinkably small in any other medium. The Third Programme, now dispersed for lack of numbers, yet spoke to audiences in scores of thousands. It is possible, even today, to address a book to only 2,000 buyers. In pre-1939 days you could 'come home' on an edition of 750 copies. This is surely a factor of great importance in matters of scholarship and in technology, and it is these freshets of culture which become finally the great rivers of civilized thought.

Finally printed communication at the hands of a competent and sensitive author makes an impact in a superior degree. There is a subtlety about the use of words in print, a flavour and a style, especially in the realms of creative writing, which has no rival. Despite the success of *The Forsyte Saga*, visual attempts to present great works of fiction are failures, and often they can only be brought to life by the injection of a musical dimension.[2] You often hear a person claim that a book has changed his life; but

[2] 'Television is a great little old medium for making you feel you are right in there knowing about art. Or at any rate artists. It's

you have not yet heard of a person whose life has been changed by a television programme.

We can claim then that, because of their physical properties, books are convenient; because of their economics they can be made for small publics; because of their manner of content they communicate uniquely.

---

all a massive con trick. As the past week has shown, yet again, you don't learn much about football from watching a documentary on George Best, about sculpture from watching a cultural item or two on Arthur Dooley, or about poetry from watching an Omnibus on John Clare. The most you get is a bit of candyfloss about the artists. And I have my doubts even about that.' Maurice Wiggin, *Sunday Times*, March 1970.

[2]

The Entrepreneurs

Many of the activities of publishing are mysterious, and some are thought glamorous. The most romantic type to the outsider is the publisher who deals in headline literary 'properties'. He is the only publisher recognizable by the general public because he is the publisher he reads about in the daily papers and the gossip columns. If such a publisher hears at a party that General Ballistic-Jordon is about to retire he surprises him with an offer of, say, £5,000 by way of advance royalties for his life-story. He is directed to the literary agent whom the eminent General has already, and unexpectedly, honoured with the exploitation of his well-spent life; for he explains that, as a Service man, he has no head for business and would rather not talk about it. His agent, however, does not share his sensitivity and talks to such purpose that a much larger sum appears on the contract.

It is real money by any standards, and if the publisher is experienced in this kind of work his stake may not be the gamble it appears. Providing the manuscript, though not yet written, is warranted to contain the necessary modicum of revelation the publisher knows that he can expect a wide sale (and massive reviewing) of the book in its original edition, to which must be added such rights as appertain to book clubs, paperbacks, and so on, with a possible cut in the subsidiary rights, ranging from first serial rights in *The Times* or the *Sunday Times* to fourth serial rights in the *Cornish Echo* or *Hampshire Globe and*

Advertiser. He may also enjoy a small share in translation rights, though he will be excluded from the American rights by the agent. The publisher bears in mind, moreover, that the General's is but one of the many books he will produce in the immediate future, that he owns both swings and roundabouts and that he is also dealing in his reputation, image and imprint. So he sleeps soundly enough, as often as not in New York as in London.

Such publishers are the large general publishing houses. They are the descendants of the Victorian grandees who 'did' Dickens, Marie Corelli, Disraeli, Lord Lytton, Mrs Humphrey Ward and the great adventurers, explorers and politicians of their time. In their announcement lists they surround General Ballistic-Jordon, as a whale among minnows, with the memories of writers, philosophers, and other lesser folk, some internationalized coffee-table books on art and history, and a few 'scholarly' books of instant history. They generally possess a best-selling novelist or two acquired at auction, writing books against advances on account. A couple of thousand pounds would be regarded as a fair advance for a best-selling novelist's unborn masterpiece, in this case rigidly excluding serial rights which often fetch in excess of that sum for the 'right property', an apt description. The list of such a publisher would include many other books picked up *en route* and will usually embody a thriller section, a romance department, as constant features, and perhaps a children's book section composed of the middle-class adventure stories and some anthropomorphic titles for the tots.

There are a dozen or more publishers operating on a substantial scale in this field, with some junior rivals. To them the literary agents bring their prize exhibits, with perhaps a few younger writers ripe for development. It is all harmless enough, provides volume for the Trade, and engaged in it you may be elected to the Garrick or Saville Clubs. It can be a little worrying at times, when, as happens, an advance of a hundred thousand pounds [*sic*] is made on a 'treatment' with the main hope of repayment hingeing on a deal in subsidiary rights; and it is always hell for Sales Managers.

Neither is it the healthiest of trades. The continuous round of parties, lunches, intercontinental travel, leaves its mark on the toughest physiques. The executives of such firms are jumpy, and on entering a room immediately reach for a drink. While they are talking to one person they glance about and part of their attention is elsewhere, as if they anticipate an attack from the flank or the stealthy approach of nemesis. Their permanent contenders are the literary agents, and to see such a publisher and a literary agent at lunch is akin to watching the courtship of the praying mantis. They need each other but one must attempt to consume the other. The rise in power of the literary agent is shown by the amount paid (as in the case of Ballistic-Jordon) in advances, reaching figures at times which no party to the agreement believes will be covered. On such occasions the publisher is gratified only by the addition of a famous name to his list.

These large publishers, skimming the cream of the manuscripts, and paying a heavy price, do not, as we have said, complain, and their profit-and-loss accounts do not indicate imminent bankruptcy, though they call for a good head for heights and depths, since results can vary dramatically from year to year. It is significant that this kind of publisher does not necessarily live from the physical sale of books but from the sale of reprint and other rights; were he deprived of these his accounts would often show losses. Nor must we be misled by profit-and-loss accounts, for whether a publisher shows a profit or a loss depends, on paper at least, on his valuation of stock. This book cannot be a guide to publishers' accounts (which, in principle, are the same as anyone's accounts) but it should be pointed out that if a stock of 10,000 copies of Ballistic-Jordon's *My War* left over at the end of a year is valued at 10s. a volume, at cost, or £5,000 in total, this would be reflected in the profit-and-loss account as a profit; but if, in a fit of pessimism, the books are written down to £1,000 in value, a loss of £4,000 is shown. A high valuation will gratify the collector of taxes, since he will be richer by the tax on £4,000, more so since he collects his profit before the books have been sold.

The largest and most traditional group of publishers, set in opposition to the journalistic or cheque-book kind, are called 'general publishers'. Despite this appellation they are *sui generis*. Often started by men of humble origin, little capital and much resource, and beginning mostly in the nineteenth century, they betray their origins by the solidity rather than the brilliance of their catalogues; indeed, up till recently they cultivated a genteel shabbiness of accommodation, much as did Victor Gollancz: 'I don't want authors to think I am making a fortune.' The names of Macmillan, Hodder, Dent, Longman, Harrap come to mind. They stand by their back lists and could make profits if they published no new titles a year because of the persistence of sale of certain books or series launched many years ago and, though not advertised in the press, known to the Trade as 'bread and butter lines'. It is a fact that such publishers can issue more new editions than new books in a season.

The backbone of such a general list can be various and

its architecture fascinating. There are books of fiction, poetry, essays, children's books (some of which you will have read as a child). A number of well-established scholarly books will appear in the list, ranging from classical texts to books on history, art and the sciences. The occasional title will secure adoption as required reading for professional or examination purposes—Gray's *Anatomy*, for example, has recently celebrated its centenary and Banister Fletcher's *History of Architecture* is in its seventeenth revised edition. Scattered throughout the pages of their catalogues are such practical books as *How to Catch Coarse Fish* or *British Birds* (or *Snails*, or *Mosses*, or *Snakes*), all at lower prices than elsewhere because they were originally produced many years ago. Such practical books may rise to the heights of an Oxford Dictionary or sink to the level of a non-book, a ready reckoner or calculator. These firms are a living demonstration of the fact that in publishing the first score of years are the worst.

Several of these older publishers include in their catalogues libraries of classical reprints of English literature. No royalties are paid on such titles though editorial fees are generally incurred (copyright subsists for fifty years after an author's death or a book's publication) and edited texts are copyright—many a pirate has tripped over this one. It is commonly thought that 'out of royalty' publishers are on to a good thing, but this is not necessarily so. In series certain titles, a few, tend to sell quickly, but most will sell slowly and are therefore unprofitable; and rival editions exist. It is to the eternal discredit of those handing out titles that in all the sixty years of *Everyman's Library* no single honour has ever been bestowed on its editors and sponsors, who have kept hundreds of titles in print almost irrespective of whether it was or was not profitable to do so.

Traditional publishers rely little upon literary agents and General Ballistic-Jordon's agents would not have knocked upon their doors. Old connexions, recommendations, bring in many of their books, and, as each publisher becomes known for his special interests, proposals may arrive on his desk from writers or scholars in those fields. But the most fruitful source of books arises from having ideas and proposing them to authors. For every idea several of these proposals may fail, if only for the reason that those who will write often don't know and those who do know won't write. When idea and author meet to produce a book of importance the publisher's pleasure is intense, for he is fulfilling his destiny—his name may live in shadowy association with that of his author. As we note elsewhere, some publishers employ scouts or advisers to keep them in touch with current thought but I know of no substitute for a good memory for published books, a lively inquiring mind, and a willingness to talk on all subjects to all men while being expert on none. A gregarious habit of life is desirable—a publisher cannot live in a vacuum.

It must be admitted that the creation of a long-term publishing business is not easy today. There are too many publishers and they have not the climatic advantages of the late nineteenth century, when a need for improvement had been created by the Education Act of 1870, and that need could be satisfied by producing books (incredible as it sounds) at a penny a copy. Nor do bookshops keep extensive standard stock as they once did and titles tend to die more quickly; it is extremely difficult to establish a title as 'bread and butter' stock. Both opportunity and fulfilment came to the publishers and bookshops of earlier days. It is to the paperback market (perhaps I should say the Penguin market) that one must look today for opportunity and its fulfilment in our own time. A combination of technical factors in book production plus editorial interests in social history, politics and science has produced a list, with the Pelican imprint, of considerable dimensions and impact. Much of its extent is still the product of hardback publishing, traditionally fathered. The Penguin effort is an Everest among paperbacks, in extent and in selection, without peer or rival among paperback publishers, as *Everyman* was in its day. Nor is it possible today to start publishing on a tiny capital and large credit, nor compete in the market with books set and plated when printing costs were low. Commerce apart, one also has the impression that all the books likely to fill a public need have already been published. This would be the pessimistic view and a case can be made out for the idea that every generation creates its own needs in books. Changes in scholarship, amounting almost to revolution, create ample opportunities: it is a fact, to give a single instance, that archaeology has grown from a folklore to a science in the life of our middle-aged man of today, and archaeological publishing has burgeoned. New social attitudes, new moralities, the very frustrations of a younger generation: these should generate material for books and provide the 'traditional' publisher with opportunities, if the money is there, and a willingness to wait. It is arguable that the major obstacle to 'real' publishing is the change in retail attitudes and this we will discuss in a later chapter. It may be thought that the Oxford and Cambridge University Presses have a very special, privileged and subsidized position, but this is not so. They are, in fact, very traditional publishers who, despite obligation to publish work of a scholarly and uncommercial kind, manage to make profits at something like the level of their commercial rivals. All that has been said of traditional publishing is applicable to their cases, only more so, for they cannot involve themselves in sensational publishing. What they have to support them is a mass of set school books, bibles, dictionaries and works of reference. The Oxford University Press is also a top-of-the-league publisher of children's books.

We are now nearing the boundaries of technical and educational publishing. This is a matter of professional expertise at high level. In a general publishing house technical and educational publishing is the preserve of the director, who understands, for instance, what a book called *Dipole Radiation in the Presence of a Conducting Half-Space* is about. Such a director will know of the teaching syllabuses surrounding his subjects and will commission suitable manuscripts from teachers. Into these special fields we cannot venture here except to remark that, once entrenched (which is not easy), you can stay for life. The textbook director may then have the dubious pleasure of observing his annotated Shakespeare still being prescribed for the eleven-year-olds of Equatorial Africa, or his Latin primer, published fifty years ago, still selling tens of thousands of copies a year. Naturally younger publishers hunger for such 'adoptions'. They often make energetic, and futile, efforts to penetrate such lush (though cut-price) pastures, but their opportunity seems to be arriving with the new teaching methods, and the new subjects, now being advocated by radical educationists.

I have so far mentioned, first, the comparatively simple, or cheque-book, type of publishing, which could also be called journalism-in-cover, since it also tends to follow

the news. Thus if hijacking is the concern of newspapers
very little time will pass before a novel with that theme
appears; if political deviation is in the news, six books on
the subject, fiction and non-fiction, will shortly appear.
In the sphere of personal notoriety the example *par excellence* of a man under pressure to make news, and a book,
is Donald Crowhurst. Second, I have mentioned the more
complex traditional general publishing, but this is not to
say that the more traditional publishers are not trying to
'go contemporary' or that the 'go-go' publishers are ignor-
ing traditional fields. Whatever the architecture, many-
mansioned or many-splendoured, these two main types
represent the publishing character as it is generally under-
stood among literate readers. Faber and Faber is a name
worth noting as being firmly founded on traditional princi-
ples in recent years with yet a flair for the contemporary
in poetry, drama and fiction.

The influx of big money, the interest of major printers
or newspaper proprietors, has created a new style of post-
war publishing as a department in other activities. They
think big and to justify their size, their capital expenses,
their crushing overheads, they must think in terms of
millions of pounds of turnover, in editions of scores of
thousands. They are computerized and often live in tower
blocks, at which staff arrive and leave with frequency.
They must streamline their books in terms of content and
design, and they cannot tolerate idiosyncrasy. They tend
to produce books in batches of titles rather than singles.
Theirs is the striking contrast to the publishing image as
a 'cottage industry'. Their need for turnover is such that
they have to be continually offering bargains and fiddling
with price structures. If a traditional publisher tries to
match book to buyer they match book to market in a

blanket operation. Many of their books are indeed bargains and, as a result, swamp the shelves of multiple stores, more so since they are generous with trade discounts. It would be easy to dismiss this kind of publishing as vapid and without character, but it does perform a useful educational purpose, as do fortnightly part-publications, in areas untouched by the traditionalists. These merchandisers have significantly increased book sales at a level far more desirable than much of paperback publishing.

A type of publishing which has something in common with this merchandising but is aimed at a higher cultural level has grown with the development of pictorial litho or gravure printing. This publishing operation is known in the Trade as 'internationalizing' or 'co-publishing'. Its inception and promotion is conceived as half-packaging and half communication, and, because the emphasis is on illustration rather than text, there exists a considerable potential in foreign editions. It has been called 'coffee-table' publishing and Geoffrey Grigson has referred to it as 'Frankfurt-produced cultural hold-alls'. It has given good returns to its reader-viewers in the form of conspectuses of art, science and history of high physical quality at most reasonable prices.

The production and sales staff in such publishing are early in the fray to reach massive printings in pooled editions of the illustrations, looking for a profitable sale even before publication.

Of this kind of publishing Tom Rosenthal, of Thames and Hudson, naturally does not stint his praise: 'This is creative publishing in the sense that the perfect subject has been allied to the perfect author or group of authors. A text has been produced which has the ring of the true standard work about it, whether it is a single internationally-acknowledged expert or whether it is a team of fourteen of the world's leading archaeologists each writing about that early civilization which is his own speciality. These are books which, allied with top-class illustration material, become not only objects of art themselves, but also valuable works of reference and educational importance. Had a publisher in any one of the countries which eventually published *A Concise History of Modern Painting* embarked upon this book by himself, he would have found that the number of copies he could reasonably expect to sell in his own country would have cost anything from £5 to £10 each, and since the book would thus have been too expensive, those copies would not have sold. If you add up the quantities that can be sold in a group of countries you come up with something like a prospective sale of 200,000. Thus you can print the expensive part of the book—that is the hundred colour plates and the 485 black-and-white illustrations—all at once and then reproduce the cheap part—that is the text—in all the languages one after another. Consequently all the participating countries were able to publish this book at a price not much greater than that of a good novel, and less than that of a good biography. For almost the first time a heavily illustrated art book with a very tough-minded text was sold all over the world in quantities one would normally associate with a best-selling popular writer.'[1]

Occasionally the publishing scene is enlivened by the appearance of a sponsored book. Sponsorship is usually from concerns outside the book trade and can take various forms: a guarantee to buy copies, a contribution towards production costs, or payment of editorial and authorship costs. The result can be some very successful books,

[1] *Books:* National Book League, No. 343, 1962.

notably the Shell range of publications and *The Guinness Book of Records*. But finally these books have succeeded on sheer merit, generating sales and low prices. The *genre* is regarded by the bookshops with some suspicion, that if a publisher is not willing to back a book with his own money there must be something wrong with it. Most publishers will hesitate to publish books financed from outside the Trade and even the books I have mentioned met, at first, a cool reception. Nor will a publisher usually accept a book paid for by the author, and for the same reason. The exception will be the work of scholarship without a commercial market and which, but for some form of subsidy, either from the author or a learned society, will not be published.

What is at present a minor form of activity in the world of publishing (and perhaps an insidious one) is gaining some ground. This is the actual production of books by a unit outside a publishing office. If you have some ideas and a genius for producing dummies there may be a future here, for its beauty from the producer's point of view is that you need no capital except that required to open an office and that you are not seriously involved in risk. For the publisher to whom you take the book, if enamoured, will order a whole edition complete and pay more or less on delivery. It calls for a good deal of nerve on the part of the buying publisher, who can be faced equally with success or failure.

The fourth kind of publishing which has grown to avalanche proportions in post-war days is, of course, paperback publishing. In choice there is an incredible range of 40,000 titles from the best in Penguin to the worst in sexology and associated horrors. It is not part of my brief to describe the methods used in selling paperbacks, either wholesale or to retailers, or, for that matter, through newsagents' shops, for this is a blanket coverage all on its own. The part is less important than the whole and the books are sold in mass almost irrespective of title. As with part-publications the great thing is to get the retailer to place a high initial order and then allow inertia to play its part, for, once the impact of heavy promotion abates, sales can be allowed to fall away until the point of finish or withdrawal is reached. My own experience in this matter is limited, but I was astonished to sell certain titles to a paperback publisher and find that he did not intend to reprint once the first edition was sold out; and he cheerfully at this stage let the rights revert to me. Sales initiative with paperbacks resides with the publisher, for the retailer will order in grosses and he will expect a new consignment of assorted authors and assorted titles when he returns his unsolds and asks for more.

Despite the publicity associated with paperbacks their sales still form a minor part of the book trade—perhaps 20 per cent. It derives in large part from hard-cover publishing, and most of the 'egghead' paperbacks would not be possible without the precedent of a hard-cover edition which will bear the original cost. Paperback publishing is, on the whole, less a publishing than a marketing operation in an area of distribution not accessible by traditional outlets. With the exception of *Penguin, Pelican* or *Pan,* who are traditional publishers at heart and in method, it provides for most books a passing surge of sales, and is not concerned with selling a particular book to a particular person.

The current success of paperback publishing is due in part to price disparity, but is also due to a new social climate and new ideas of design and access. These books, following the Penguin example, stripped off their aloofness and began to push their way into the face of the passer-by or, according to the *Financial Times*, 'grasp at the passer-by with a prostitute's claw'. They looked gay and appetizing, and they went with beards, long pullovers and suede shoes. At last it seemed books and low life were in conjunction. If paperbacks are bought and not read this is no disadvantage so far as the Trade is concerned: it is sufficient that fashion decrees the buying of paperbacks, and, as Arnold Bennett remarked on another occasion, their very presence is enough. The paperback division of publishing is, of course, becoming overcrowded, but the strong firms will survive. I believe also in the survival power of good books and that a taste for good literature, and the arts, is not easily set aside. It is for publishers and booksellers to see that the appetite grows by what it feeds on.

Except in parts of the field of entertainment, the dominance of books does not seem to be seriously challenged as yet. Indeed, the Trade is in ferment. Turnover figures continue to rise; more titles than ever are being produced. The growth of sales is indeed surprising, from £10,500,000 in 1939 to £140,000,000 in 1969. We can say that, making allowances for the fullest inflation, it has more than doubled. The Trade's financial health must, however, be measured by the sale of an economic quantity of each title. In 1937 the sales arose from 17,137 new editions and titles; in 1969 from 30,000 titles, and division between one figure and another gives perhaps a misleading result, since most book sales are not those currently published but arise from a huge backlog of *Books in Print*. This reference work, of immense proportions, lists 200,000 back-list books at present available. A glance at its congested pages puts the current fashions into a perspective of 500 years.

But this growth also exposes the basic dichotomy of the Trade. Inflation has reached the point when it is difficult to finance expansion from existing cash sources. More firms are 'going public' and growth is being financed by the merchant banks, the industrialists, the invading Americans. Cash obtained from these sources is expensive. Shareholders clamour for increased dividends, and are not particularly concerned with what is sold to get them; and merchant banks must have a margin above their borrowing rate, and look for a return of 20 per cent. They are, moreover, not interested in small businesses and tend to think of conglomerates and mergers: anything less than a loan of six figures is not interesting to them. Inevitably they push their publishers in the direction of the literary property market, the immediately profitable and expendable book which carries within it exciting paperback and visual potentialities—one such first novel of the right recipe is claimed to have earned a quarter of a million pounds in sales before a single member of the public or a single critic had read it.

Half of London's (and New York's) publishers are trying to live off this type of merchandise with its immediate profits; the rest still believe that enduring prosperity comes from slow-selling back-list 'quality' books; and there are naturally many publishers trying to make the best of both worlds. This is the present division of the Trade and which you choose to be in is largely a matter of your temperament. It illustrates perfectly Chesterton's distinction between a man who wants a book to read and a man who wants to read a book.

The Creators

It is perhaps appropriate, at the end of our outline of the architecture of publishing, to look more closely at the way in which books make their way from author to announcement list. Very few manuscripts submitted to publishers from the public at large achieve acceptance and publication. On receipt of a titillating letter a publisher will hasten to welcome the sight of a manuscript, because there is no living publisher who does not feel that this might be the moment of discovery for which he has lived and struggled in the twilight for years. Alas very few such manuscripts are decently presented (some bearing, as an editor of mine once remarked, no more relation to a book than a heap of scrap-iron to a sword), and, with rare exceptions, they turn out to be of negligible value. The notion that works of genius float around for years from rejection to rejection can be dismissed. They can mostly be rejected on grounds of bad writing, bad arrangement, lack of freshness and originality.

Nearly all agreements, and eventual publication, are published by arrangement, between agent and publisher or directly between publisher and author. The agent does some kind of selection and will not submit manuscripts of an impossible kind. Since agents, quite reasonably, give the larger houses first choice the smaller non-fiction publisher usually gets most of his books by marrying author to subject. This is creative publishing. He thinks up an idea and offers it to an author; and once in four or five times his offer is accepted, often not for money, since usually an amateur author will find that his profession pays better, but perhaps because there is something about authorship—your name in print: 'He must be an authority —he has written a book about it.' Some of the larger non-fiction houses maintain advisers at universities and technical colleges, paying them an annual honorarium for introductions and ideas; but literary advisers are a mixed blessing.

The author-publisher relationship has grown up over several hundred years and has, more often than not, been an acrimonious one. When one party to an agreement has, or appears to have, access to money and another is dependent or supplicant, mutual respect is hardly nourished. The public impression that the publisher—or, before the Trade became divided, the bookseller—is usually the offending party can be ascribed to the fact that the author is practised in self-expression and the publisher is not. Resentment is an occupational disease with many authors (witness John Dryden's portrait of Jacob Tonson, his publisher); publishers, inured to anonymity, become philosophers.

Professional authorship is a declining occupation in terms of writing books exclusively and of deriving income from book publication. There are probably today fewer than fifty people whom one can call bookmen in the old meaning, in the sense of being Somerset Maugham, Hugh Walpole, Kipling, Wells, Hardy, Walter Scott or R. L. Stevenson. Looking at these names one enters the world of professional bookmen. They catered for a world anxious to read their books unalloyed by cinema, radio, television. If you were not a novelist of fame you were still a professional; you wrote books and you were passing rich, and rather distinguished, on £500 a year. Today this race is nearly extinct, replaced by authors who write scripts, work up ideas for television or cinema, do journalism or public relations pamphlets for industrial concerns. They exploit their word-talent in many ways. They write books incidentally and for the subsidiary values arising from them. They face the fact that today you cannot generally make £1,000 a year from writing books, and they find alternative though still literary employment. Moreover, the tide of literary flow has changed direction. Up to thirty years ago the British writer spoke to the whole English-speaking world and the most respectable American lists reflected the British literary scene. Now the trend is reversed and a high proportion of British best-sellers come from America.

Let us imagine that you are writing a book. It is an advantage to write a book in the first place, for it is the parent of subsidiary rights and gives status. Film magnates, for instance, still live in considerable love of the printed word in a hard binding. When you are part of the way through the writing you see a literary agent or a publisher, show him what you have done, and you may get a contract which pays you a 10 per cent royalty on the published price and an advance on account of that royalty. If your publisher has hopes of a considerable sale of your work he will, at this stage, get to work on serialization or featurization prospects in a popular weekly or Sunday newspaper. If this comes off you are not precluded from seeing your work in a provincial journal or even serialized in Australia or South Africa: for serialization is divided into first, second and perhaps even third serial rights.

Your book is published and meets with some success (sells 5,000 copies) which your publisher makes out to be a large one. He tries, or has tried, to interest a book club in your work; he tries to interest the B.B.C. or a magazine using instalments, or a paperback concern in a later reprint. He will, if he has the rights, offer it to America; perhaps translation rights overseas. If he is offered 10 guineas for the Thai rights and £50 for the Japanese rights he closes at once before they change their minds and wonders when he will get his money. The net begins to spread out, catching both the large whales and tiny sticklebacks.

You may get interested in trying to adapt your book to a dramatic medium, for, as we have remarked, new kinds of communication are being developed and literary property is drifting away from mere book publishing into a complex pattern of marketing in which the form of the commodity is considerably changed.

All this is, of course, a kind of dream. The majority of books are born, struggle faintly and fall into limbo—only one in three or four pays its production costs, and one in a hundred gets a sniff at serial or paperback rights. A book has to be in the climate of its time to be that successful, as I have already indicated; it is not enough for commercial success that it shall have intrinsic literary or creative merit. One of the saddest experiences in publishing is to glance at a big seasonal issue of the *Bookseller* of the previous year, and grieve for the high hopes which the passage of twelve months has dispelled. Perhaps the greatest mortality is among the books intended for the general reader; the least among those of minority appeal.

It is true today that the majority of authors in the catalogue of a general publisher are what we might call occasional authors. They derive the larger part of their income from other sources. They write for public information and edification; they write for fame; they do not write for money. In these circumstances they are easier to deal with financially; by and large they are satisfied with a 10 per cent royalty (and if they were not, this kind of scholarly publishing would not be possible); they are often surprisingly pleased that even a thousand or two people will read their books. Unfortunately these authors tend to run to length and complicated illustration, have little idea of what is practical in printing processes, and editors have to be called in to process their work.

I do not want to divide authors into the 'creative' author and the scholar or disseminator of information. This kind of distinction in the world in which we live is a false one; the mind ranges variously in many fields and at a certain point of thought it is difficult to tell when information becomes creation. The division between artist and craftsman is a modern snobbery unknown until recent times, and Dr Johnson was both a critic and a compiler of dictionaries.

Loyalty to one's publisher, providing there is reasonable trust on both sides, is a desirable state of affairs. Our author may well find that his publisher will not only listen to him but suggest book ideas himself; and it is possible, with concessions and consideration all round, that a fruitful author-publisher relationship may develop. Moreover a publisher is inclined to be more interested in an author than in a book; and it is common talk in the Trade that authors who change publishers inevitably arrive at a point when no publisher has enough investment in him to promote his books as a whole. H. G. Wells was a prime example of an author who went always to the highest bidder, and found at the end of his life that most of his books were out of print, and no publisher would undertake, could undertake, a 'collected edition'.

Literary agents are today an inescapable feature of the landscape and, having arrived in strength, they can be useful and necessary; it is desirable that a *modus operandi* should be arranged. Certain publishers live hand-in-glove with literary agents and could not survive for a moment without them. They are necessary when dealing with desirable literary properties, and they are useful in dealing with subsidiary rights for books which have that kind of potential. A successful 'creative' writer who has been writing novels for some years really needs an agent to deal with his business problems. Whether an agent is useful at lower levels of popularity and complexity is open to doubt. An agent has to pay regard to the fact that his return is a commission on sales, and he is unlikely to make great effort to sell rights which will bring him in, say, a couple of pounds: whereas both author and publisher have more than money in mind, reputation for example, and they appreciate that sales and income arise from innumerable small transactions. The result of this attitude is that an agent will sometimes withhold rights which he does not intend to exploit, or is unlikely to exploit, from a publisher.

Let us look at the kind of life led by a less successful author trying to earn his living by writing (and there are not many of the more successful kind). He produces a book each year. Published at, say 35*s.*, he sells in all 3,000 copies on a 10 per cent royalty and receives something like £500 from this part of the transaction. A small edition of his book is exported to America and from this he will receive 10 per cent of the price paid by the American publisher. Sales of this kind to America are usually disposed of at a discount of 60 per cent of the British published price, so that he will receive 10 per cent of 14s. a copy, and on 2,000 copies this will come to £140. If an American publisher actually produces the book and pays a royalty on the American published price our author's income is much improved, to as much as £500 on a 2,000–3,000 sale. Of course, there are the prospects of paperbacking, of serialization, of broadcasting, but the total return of about £1,000–£1,200 is not exactly exciting. Contrast this with the returns made to General Ballistic-Jordon as chronicled earlier. This disparity arises from the publisher's estimate of the public (and the reviewers') interest. It has but small relation to importance, significance, and should not be taken too much to heart. Most English classics were remaindered when originally published. Between the two extremes we may note that the one-book amateur, a master of his subject, may receive, in a longer term and at a higher price, as much as a couple of thousand pounds for his work, and the successful school textbook author, even on a very low royalty, may earn an income amounting to several thousand pounds a year.

[4]

The Makers and Marketers

I was until recently in charge of an organization which included a publishing house. After many years it was thought desirable that a diagnosis of its activities should be made. A firm of business consultants was called in. They did well, and intelligently, until they came to the creative side of our publishing activities. At this point their criteria broke down. They persisted in treating the business of publishing as other businesses. They said that our organization was lacking in efficiency and they recommended a vigorous weeding-out of the enthusiastic staff on which we managed.

We had to say No. Good as was their advice, we wanted to stay as publishers. That is to say, we wanted to stay in a business in which, with deliberation, we published books which we knew could not make a profit, and whose meed of success depended upon the individuals in our office. We were not engaged in selling a single product but four or five new enterprises every month; our consultants had no plan which permitted such variety.

I have already suggested that you must not, in publishing, employ people deficient in business sense. Dealing in something that nobody actually needs, and can in any case borrow, the publishing employee must conceal under his long hair a business brain. He must hear a different drummer. So let us consider how one may walk with angels nor lose the common touch. Let us consider also that we are dealing in a subject of some complexity; that no operation goes completely smoothly; that processes overlap and fuse and that a high publishing asset is to be able to see a progressing pattern in the operations now to be described; and for that there is hardly a substitute for possessing a good memory for detail.

I have made the point earlier that manuscripts of a publishable kind do not just float into a publisher's office. With authors and agents he usually has to hunt for them or 'create' them. In a small publishing office the managing director himself does this job: it is the key to the character of his list. When a manuscript arrives it is not, as is generally supposed, sent straight to a printer. The book must first be passed by a sub-editor, or someone who will 'go through it'. For the following reasons: (1) it may not be the book ordered; (2) it may be too long, too short, badly written and unreadable, or inaccurate or poorly organized; (3) it may be scandalous, libellous or plagiaristic. When he signs the agreement the author declares that it is none of these things and that he will reimburse you for your trouble or against proceedings brought against you; but it is almost certain that he will not, has not, the means to do so. So you employ editors and, if your subject is 'hot', you employ a solicitor. Some publishers edit to a 'house style', have their own ideas about spelling, punctuation, capitalization, consistency; it is often based on the Oxford University Press's *Rules for Compositors* and their *Authors' and Printers' Dictionary*, on the *Oxford Dictionary* and *Fowler's Modern English Usage*.

In the middle-to-large publishing house 'editor', as a term, has wider usage. He is the publisher's contact with the world of letters and learning; he has ideas or his contacts have ideas and his object is to see that these ideas, if thought publishable, are put into manuscript and made ready for printing. Various publishers have various editors (sometimes elevated by the term 'editorial director'). A scholarly publisher values university contacts; a merchandising publisher values contacts with literary agents; a socialite publisher likes editors in that swim. All successful editors have contacts, imagination, powers of persuasion, if only because the suggestion to an amateur author that he should write 100,000 words is rather frightening, and because writing a book calls for a stamina not commonly available.

In the larger publishing offices the editorial conferences occur once a week or a fortnight. Here usually the editors and directors decide what is publishable. The pros and cons are argued of policy and style, and the anticipated published prices of the books and the numbers to be printed. The manuscripts are now accompanied by a rough estimate of production costs. At the other extreme are publishers who will decide, without consultation, what they want to publish in pursuance of their settled interests.

As one who has attended upon many decisions as to whether a book shall or shall not be published, I can say that the reasons for publishing a book, apart from the hope of making profits, are many and various. They may be set down as follows:

(1) Because the author's books have been previously published by the firm.

(2) As a matter of 'policy' and in line with 'the character of the firm's list'.

(3) 'As a service to scholarship or literature' (often serve the personal interests of the managing director).

(4) Because the author is 'a nice chap' (a friend).

(5) Because 'if we don't, someone else will'.

(6) Because we must get a list together for next year, and because it will help to 'cover the overheads'.

All are good reasons for publishing in certain circumstances, providing they are accepted with eyes open. In my own case, in the least objective of publishing houses, we sometimes accept a book and cost it to make a small loss or break even. We call this 'realistic', while hoping that it won't be.

Here I must touch on the delicate subject of the literary adviser. It is the practice of some firms to appoint an eminent and supposedly influential person to make contact with geniuses and encourage them to work for his firm. While this tradition is a respectable one (and the name of Edward Garnett stands pre-eminent in this field), younger or poorer publishers need not despair if only for the reason that, sooner or later, if you employ an adviser you must take his advice. Most publishers eventually dispose of their literary advisers (as opposed to readers and contact men) with a sigh of relief. They are too human in some respects; too inhuman in others. They indulge their fancies; they help their friends; and by contrast they often take a high view of their responsibilities towards literature, recommending books that are a sales manager's nightmare and rejecting those which are his delight.

Once a contract has been signed the editorial department prepares the manuscript for the printers, arranges the necessary illustrations, in itself quite often an arduous and time-consuming operation. The manuscript can now pass to the production manager. If your editor is the key person in a cultural sense, your production manager is the key person in an economic sense. A publisher is often asked how much it costs to produce a book. It is a question obviously with a hundred answers, but the bare cost of printing blocks, paper and binding an edition probably averages £1,200. The production manager in a moderate-sized publishing house will then have the responsibility of spending £100,000 a year. If he can save 5 per cent on this sum he is making a substantial contribution to his firm's profits. If he makes a mistake in his arithmetic he can lose irrecoverably the profit on a book. His ideas of book design will also contribute to a publisher's reputation for taste or lack of it. There is no room for doubt, for instance, that the impeccable taste of Cape or Faber (or Penguin) has contributed in a major sense to their reputation, though whether such taste is a help or a handicap in the pursuit of sales and profits is very doubtful.

The production manager submits to the publisher as close an estimate of the cost of producing a book as will enable the publisher to make final decisions: the budget. The most important of these decisions relates to the price of the book and the size of edition to be printed; and the publisher remembers that it is on the last quarter of the edition that his profits are made. The production manager will work out a speculative total edition profit, taking into account sales at normal and abnormal discounts, assuming that all copies will be sold; and he will make an estimate of the break-even point, when all costs on the edition have been covered, and when thereafter all copies sold are a clear profit. The publisher may send the estimate back to production for modification, and one well-known publisher is said to have been in the habit of doing so with an instruction to 'make it look better'.

A publisher is at one of the critical points in his career when he is looking at budgets: pricing and the length of run ('Can I sell X copies at X price?') will, apart from his choice of books to publish, make or break his profit-and-loss account. There is no doubt that successful publishers are the ones who answer the question correctly, and I have heard a publisher say that the crucial virtue is to know when to print small and when to print a large edition; for the wrong decision will either mean that the write-off in stock values at the year's end will swallow all profitability or involve high reprint costs and lower his profit. Each publisher will try to answer this question soberly from past experience, but in the majority of such decisions there is no experience, or changing markets put something of a discount on experience; and no man in the publishing trade can think objectively when faced with a book on a particular subject—his outlook is always coloured by his interest. Too often, alas, with a difficult decision, he decides to print more copies to lower a price, and it is far easier to do this than price up for a smaller run. In this bad decision his production manager, who is usually looking over his shoulder, will be quick to point out that the 'run on' price is negligible, a false assertion, since it becomes incorporated in the general body of the estimate. If the publisher cannot correlate market with price, then in theory he should abandon the enterprise; but then he goes on because by now he is caught up in a desire to publish the book, and has probably signed a contract.

Finally the acceptable price must rest on the size of the edition or 'run'. The high cost of setting and blocks is the overriding cost in small editions, up to 5,000, but becomes less important, as the initial cost is spread, on 10,000 and flattens out, at, say 20,000. On very popular books with a high conventional price, some novels for example, the margin left after production cost can be large: they are not on that account priced lower than the unpopular ones.[1]

The production manager will know what price and profit has to be set down as ideal: roughly four to five times basic production cost, ex-royalty. This relation of cost to retail price often astonishes the public, which tends to overlook the fact that a bar of chocolate or a box of matches may well cost only a twentieth of its retail price in terms of manufacture—nor is there a high speculative element in such articles. A specimen budget appears as an appendix to this book, and from this it will be seen that even the ideal position seldom produces a high profit— and the ideal position (a sell-out) is reached by only one book in every four or five.

The Production Department will ask the printer to produce a specimen page or opening, in a type and to a measure approved by the publisher. The specimen also sets out a detailed type specification. For example, this book is set in '10 on 12 pt Bell 341 to 19½ ems measure by 33 lines'. In printing shorthand this gives the typeface, its size, the amount of space between lines (leading), the length of a line, and the number of lines to a page. The pica em is the standard printing measure and equals one-sixth of an inch. The specimen will also include a 'cast-off' or estimated number of pages.

[1] Sir Stanley Unwin provides the following in *The Truth About Publishing*. If the initial cost of type setting is £200 the cost of composition will be:

£20 per copy if	10 copies are printed.
£2 per copy if	100 copies are printed.
4s. per copy if	1,000 copies are printed.
5d. per copy if	10,000 copies are printed.
½d. per copy if	100,000 copies are printed.

Here begins the struggle between printer and publisher. Every item which varies from the original estimate is charged as an extra, and such extras are often so many and appear so inflated that the publisher has the feeling that he is paying for every breath drawn at the printer's as well as for all his own mistakes. And, at the end, too often, the number of copies produced often falls short of the number requested, and indeed required, to make the book profitable: this is known as 'reasonable wastage' by the Master Printers' Federation. The most important item on the budget is therefore a good allowance for contingencies. I should also note here that competitive estimates (and indeed all charges) are too often no longer that: the printer works to a costing system provided by the Master Printers' Federation and, not curiously, printers' estimates have a way of showing only small variation in total.

The organizing ability of the Production Department has to be keyed to the point that those engaged in selling the books shall have at their hands adequate samples or proofs or at least some book jackets, for it is no longer acceptable that bookshops shall decide on their requirements from the vague aspirations printed in the publishers' announcement lists. Production has also to be keyed to a time-table which takes account of publication dates, publishing seasons, and the need to bring together wrapper, paper, blocks, sheets and binding in a finished book. This, in turn, must be related to financial income balancing outgoings so that the bank cannot accuse you of 'overtrading'.

In due course, through the production manager, will come paper and binding specimens, and proofs of text and illustrations. Proofs of text will usually come first in galley—long slips of three or four pages—and then in page or 'book' form. Sometimes, with simple books uncomplicated by pictures in text, the printer will make up straight into page. All this is easy and not too expensive if the job is printed 'letterpress', that is the usual relief method; setting in Monotype (letter by letter) or Linotype (line by line), but proofs by lithography or gravure are infinitely expensive and perhaps impracticable. Since the showing of proofs is an essential part of the sales process, methods other than letterpress are not liked by the Sales Department unless the book is planned and produced a long time ahead (which won't please the company secretary) or is in a large edition, in which litho or gravure can make savings of a substantial kind. It may be that the nature of the original illustrations compels a production department to use litho or gravure to secure an excellence of result. Proofing illustrations can, even with letterpress, prove expensive if colour is being used, but this problem can be overcome if the blockmaker produces sufficient proofs for the selling job at the time of making the blocks. Decisions as to what process of reproduction is to be used, and the manufacture of blocks, are too complicated to be gone into here, and the reader must resort to his technical library, though blockmakers themselves do often give excellent advice sometimes coloured by their need to get as much work as they can.

You will note that the effort, from the very first moment of a manuscript's acceptance, is to get out some selling material in line with budget costs—for any slightest variation from the production specification will cost more. Again I emphasize that production is the big spending department as well as the most 'technical' of all departments. Upon its organizing genius largely hangs the publisher's ability to make a profit; in these circumstances it has a tendency to resist costly, and therefore unreasonable, demands from the Sales Department.

In the meantime the Sales Department has begun working. The blurbs for wrappers and announcement list are put in hand (with the author's help, though 'no more than 250 words' is something of a frustration), equally compounded of hyperbole and fact, and booksellers' and publishers' agents in all parts of the world learn that one more swan is to be launched and prepare to receive a goose. That expensive feature of modern technology, the jacket (or packaging), is begun. Time was, in my own memory, when a piece of plain brown paper protected a substantial binding; as a concession to the buyer a hole was cut in the paper covering the book's spine through which the title could, with difficulty, be perceived. Today all the resources of design and print are lavished on something which, soon after the book's appearance, may be thrown away and which usually serves to hide an inferior and aesthetically horrid binding. The reasons for the change are clear enough. Public and booksellers alike are deeply influenced by packaging in an age of eye-appeal, and it is usual and convenient for publishers to distribute proofs of the wrapper in soliciting orders and for booksellers to show them to their customers in turn. So, although it is extravagant, often costing half of the price of actual binding, it is effective.

At this stage it is the Sales Department's job (and this sometimes includes a separate Publicity Department) to see that agents overseas, and those, such as library suppliers, interested in working some months ahead, are advised of its plans. A publisher warns in stages of announcement: list, wrapper, galley, page or book proofs, to the finished job; and some publishers also send out droves of press notices to build up interest. At this point various rights and overseas editions are arranged: American rights, book club and serial rights, feature rights in press and B.B.C.

The major weapon in the publishers' armoury is the Announcement List: usually *Spring and Summer* and *Autumn and Winter*. The Publicity or Sales Department will have had a lead from the publisher or the Editorial Department as to the treatment and display of particular titles and they will try to bear in mind the books which are most likely to succeed and those which (the early fervour having vanished) must be considered as run-of-the-mill; the books about which a publisher can find something to say and the books about which he wonders how they got in at all. He will also include in his list a note of those recently published, with reviews. He will also add a note of new editions of staple books; and he will struggle to find something for his cover design a little less obvious than spring flowers and falling leaves.

In dealing with his seasonal lists he is, as I say, launching his basic attack upon the public. This is especially so with a publisher of serious books rather than merchandise. He will, in advance of publication, print many thousands (25,000 would not be an excessive figure) and send it to anyone in the world likely to buy a particular book: bookshops, public and institutional libraries, schools, universities, technical colleges, to his private mailing lists ranging from the interested layman to members of various learned societies working from the general to the particular. From this same compulsion, to reach everyone possible in as economical way as possible, springs the issue of a General Catalogue, to be produced at intervals mainly as a reference for the bookseller (and sometimes even for the publisher), and various specialist lists or subject lists: children's, music, science, history, and so on.

The seasonal list will contain a number of books for which separate prospectuses must be issued, each to be sent to a specialist public by the publisher or distributed by specialist bookshops. The publisher does not, except 'in difficulty', accept orders, but directs his customers to the bookshops.

From these major lists spring a flow of smaller material —duplicated, printed, mimeographed, or litho'd, as final reminders to trade customers and to those likely to be excited into buying or borrowing a book. A few publishers issue house organs or bulletins and some content themselves with periodic title lists.

A certain amount of free publicity is associated with dates of publishing. The Whitaker lists, in which all books are listed, are the main distributors of information. There is a weekly list in the *Bookseller* (both a publishers' and booksellers' journal), and this is cumulated into a monthly, a quarterly and an annual list; and finally jells into a massive tome called *Books in Print*, in which recent and older books in print are listed: a magnificent reference service. There is also, springing from the dispatch of a free copyright copy to the British Museum Library, a free listing in the official *British National Bibliography*, the frequent resort of public librarians in book ordering. Lately there has also sprung up a series of uniform filing cards called Pics from Whitaker, which perform a useful circularizing service, at small expense, to librarians and educational institutions. What is badly needed is an annotated, illustrated, not-too-selective, listing of new books for the general reader, not based, as bookshop catalogues often are, on a publisher's willingness to pay for entry.

I should be misleading my readers if I suggested that all publishers perform this rather complex, not to say expensive, publicity minuet. As in other directions, I write as a publisher of a characteristic type, whose selling effort is to the consumer most of the time, whose response is received through bookshops, and who does not normally reach out for the general public's interest by large advertising in the press or the probability of reviews in the press. The increasing problem with this type of publishing is reaching a special public at a reasonable price, which, with inflation all round, leaves this activity profitable only with what is called 'high unit value'—that the price of the book or group of books must make accommodation for fairly high selling cost; and this cannot be allowed in a book costing 30s. or less. You can work this out for yourself; assuming that a mailing shot costs £30 a thousand, of which £15 is postage, you can estimate that, after allowances for trade discounts, your selling cost as a publisher permits you to spend, at most, 10 per cent of your income on promotion, and the return, therefore, at £30 per 1,000 must be £300 or 200 copies of a book priced at 45s. and sold to the trade at 30s. This would seem an unbelievably high return to a mail-order expert, and is really unattainable; but publishers have no alternative but to go on doing it.

The truth is that no publisher of a general kind really knows what sells his books. It is clearly an amalgam of all promotion methods and a casting of the bread on the waters. On the whole he will tend to spend 5–7 per cent of his income on printed promotion, whether press or catalogue or prospectus. He will, if he is an old-established publisher, spend a lower percentage because his back list of books will continue to sell in some degree whether he promotes them or not.

My experience of press advertising, and if it is limited it is also based on direct selling through book clubs, is that the papers that come nearest to selling general books at a price publishers can afford to pay are the major Sundays—the *Sunday Times*, the *Observer*, the *Sunday Telegraph* and, among dailies, *The Times*, the *Daily Telegraph* and the *Guardian*. As a weekly the *New Statesman* stands high and *Books and Bookmen* is becoming a force in the book world. It is now a fact that the expansion of size and circulation of the 'heavy' Sundays has managed to attract most of the serious and regular book-buyers in the British Isles. The *Sunday Times* alone now has a circulation of nearly a million and a half. Despite this Sunday 'blanket' coverage publishers, where they advertise at all, do support other media, from the *Spectator* to such 'provincials' as the *Scotsman* and the *Glasgow Herald* in the north to the *Birmingham Post* and *Liverpool Post* further south. Among evenings the *Evening Standard* has always shown an awareness of publishing and its economics.

It must be plain to all that the mass circulation papers issued as dailies cannot have advertising value to book publishers. Advertising charges based on circulation mean that book publishers are paying high prices for wasted readers. 'The *Daily Mirror* devoted three pages to A. P. Herbert's *Hobart Paper*, equivalent to £10,000, without visibly increasing its sales; such (advertising) calculations would be misleading.'[2] Cape's have recently

[2] *Advertising in Action*, by Ralph Harris and Arthur Seldon. The Institute of Economic Affairs, 1962. This is tendentious, of course, but supports my general experience. Michael Sadleir's *Authors and the Book Trade* (Constable) is worth reading and Frank Swinnerton has also written on the subject.

'couponed' one of their books in the popular dailies, as an experiment, with the same result.

The specialized press must, of course, be favoured for publishers' advertising. For a view of the Trade and its activities there is no rival to the *Bookseller*: its seasonal bumper numbers of spring and autumn are an impressive record of energy and a depressing intimation of mortality to publishers. An advertisement in *The Times Literary Supplement* or *The Times Educational Supplement* influences not only its readers as individuals but institutional buying in general; schools and libraries in a world-wide context. In its particular field *Antiquity* will sell books on archaeology, *Popular Gardening* books on that subject and the *Angling Times* books on coarse fishing. The number of journals which exist to serve special purposes (as found in Willing's *Press Guide*) is a tribute to the depth, variety, and fecundity of British civilization; a serious publisher makes it his business to acquaint himself with many of them.

The press also performs the function of reviewing some portion of the output of publishers, and it is very welcome when it comes. Review copies are lavishly distributed to fifty or a hundred newspapers, and, since four out of five will not earn reviews, involve a massive waste. Clearly, some books need almost no promotion, since the newspapers will do it all for nothing—a volume of memoirs by Harold Macmillan, a new novel by Margaret Drabble or Iris Murdoch, any book by C. P. Snow, Geoffrey Grigson or about Max Beerbohm. Most newspapers review only these inevitable headliners, and in the 'heavies', the *Sunday Times*, the *Observer*, the *Sunday Telegraph*, the idiosyncrasies of literary editors are often frustrating to a publisher who labours for years over books of scholarship rather than books on people, on politics and opinion or fiction. Literary editors feel, properly, that is it not their business to support the book trade but to interest their readers. This must mean that a book of importance must often be counted as having only secondary value if it is about a subject on which they feel the public is indifferent or if it is not written by a notoriety. It follows that books of ephemeral value are reviewed at length, and then damned by the reviewer. Famous, too, in the Trade are the 're-viewers' books'—usually books of academic literary interest noticed at length by highbrow critics and reaching reader saturation at that stage.

The Times Literary Supplement used to be the serious publishers' stand-by. 'Well, anyway, the *T.L.S.* will review it', was the great consolation. It stood as the only comprehensive and judicial survey of publishing output, but this bastion is creaking as its proprietors push the editors for readability, for immediacy. Even here books by noisy writers are often immediately reviewed and excellent and quieter books are often noticed much later. One of the present spectacles of the Trade is the battle between its editorial staff trained in assessing scholarship—especially literary scholarship—and the insistent demands of 'immediacy'.

With a general book of excellence but little fashionable appeal there is little left to do if the reviews do not come. This is a hard conclusion for publishers but harder for authors, who feel that publishers do not advertise enough. How false is this assumption! Supposing you take six inches in serious Sunday to advertise a book: this will cost you £150. Publishers know that to spend 6 per cent of their income in promoting their books is rather more than they can afford to pay (and what other trade would spend as much?), but let us spend 10 per cent, so that if a book is published at 30s. 1,500 readers of the paper will have to go out and buy, not borrow, the book! I would say that about fifty people would buy it. It certainly does not pay to advertise at this rate, except in the case of foregone best-sellers, about which the public is only waiting to be tipped-off. In the thirties, when the leading merchandising publishers competed mightily in space-buying in the Sundays, it was thought that Victor Gollancz, the *nonpareil*, would watch the sales of his new books with a thoughtful eye, pick out those few with big potential sales, advertise them heavily, and forget the rest. Whether he made best-sellers this way is doubtful, for he is also alleged to have split his first editions half-way and printed 'Second Edition' on the second half of the run. One of his advertisements that seemed to strain credibility a little read, 'First edition sold out. Second edition printing. Third edition paper ordered.'

These are difficult facts for authors, who are often inclined to think that a publisher, having invested £1,000 in a book, has no interest in recovering that sum and will even neglect to inform booksellers of its existence. After a general book has failed to attract the attention of reviewers the publisher and author can only hope for a bit of luck: a book club choice, an American sale, perhaps, remotely, a paperback. At any rate the book goes into his stock list and will, from year to year, sell a few copies.

At the other end of the spectrum there is the book for which the market is not only perceptible but accessible. How marvellous, then, to rely on yourself! Such a book on a special aspect of archaeology can be so pinpointed as to its market that everyone interested can be reached by list or prospectus; and for the publisher it becomes a matter of making a prospective purchaser believe that it is an important book which he must have on his shelves. Or a technical book on, say, structural engineering. Every engineer in the country can be reached, almost touched, by the publisher's probing fingers. These are the books on which firms like McGraw Hill and Pergamon Press founded their fortunes and on which sensible publishers seek avidly to repair their losses on general literature.

For children's books there is much that can be done in direct promotion. All school libraries can be circularized and so can all public libraries, accounting certainly for more than half of the trade done. There are, moreover, several magazines devoted to children's reading, and these do a good sorting-out job and seem to miss little of importance, though perhaps over-given to fiction and whimsy. (*The Cow Who Lived on Buttercups* is praised as exercising the imagination while a book on space travel is ignored!) *The School Librarian* is outstanding among these, as the organ of the School Libraries Association, and there are Margery Fisher's *Growing Point* and *Junior Bookshelf*. *The Times Literary Supplement* and *The Times Educational Supplement* devote special numbers to children's books and cover an enormous amount of ground though obsessively fancy and fiction; non-fiction (so-named) bringing up the rear. One is tempted to think that if adult books were as well surveyed—and in as liberal a fashion—publishers would have little to complain of. Moreover, children's books do not die quickly, and, once established as favourites, they are hard to shift—you have only to think of Mary Norton and Enid Blyton to appreciate this point. The Publishers' Association has a Children's Book Group (and so has the Library Association) which organizes an annual Children's Book Show, awards medals and has other activities.

We must talk about publishers' travellers, or representatives as they like to be called. In bookish terms they are an unrepresentative lot; it seems to be a condition of their calling that they should be mildly contemptuous of the books they have to sell. The traveller who, on being reproached, retorted that it was bad enough to have to sell the books without being obliged to read them was faithful after his fashion. They are daily exposed to the bookseller's jaundiced attitude to the never-ceasing flow of books, and they are liable to become infected with the philosophy that a good book is a fast-selling book and a bad book is one that hangs fire for a day to two; and the bookseller is quick to point out that the books at present being offered fall into the second category. Literary taste is certainly a dubious qualification for a traveller; it can result in an enthusiasm for his own taste in books and a lack of it for others. Most publishers plump for a kind of neutral representation, assisted by an indestructible cheerfulness, a course which commends itself on the whole to the bookseller.

Personally I have always found it hard to reproach the publishers' traveller. At least he has the courage to wake up each morning and face with fortitude the prospect of a round of calls, receiving everything from kindness to apathy and even hostility; and sometimes finishing the day, in certain 'graveyard' areas, with a complete blank. At which a reproachful note from the comfort of the sales manager's office will very likely soon reach him.

These representatives, swarming over England in their hundreds, are no doubt a great nuisance to bookshops, but it seems likely that but for their existence few bookshops would carry a basic representation of books, and that space intended for them would soon be ruthlessly occupied by other merchandise. Such a potent sales weapon in the hands of publishers is unlikely to be superseded or abandoned, and survives every obstacle and discouragement. It is gratifying to report that representatives are generally well paid and that quite often the senior traveller receives, after the managing director, the best remuneration in the house. He is paid in varying ways, carefully worked out to give him a basic living and an incentive to live more luxuriously: a salary, expenses and a commission on orders. Overseas representatives are also employed, notably in the British Commonwealth. In the larger houses there are often branches in Australia and in South Africa; elsewhere, agents are paid usually a commission on all orders emanating from their territory.

To the unfortunate Sales Department falls finally the job of raising some cash by remaindering unsuccessful books, usually at one-tenth of their published price, and to be sold at a half to a third of published price. Books of information and scholarship are in demand here, but fiction is unsaleable. When I say 'unsuccessful books' I can recall, of course, good books of which too many have been printed; or books successful in their first edition and which have been optimistically reprinted when often the sales suddenly fall away.

Exports are traditionally an important part of a book publisher's turnover, and the total trade percentage is to-day in the region of 44 per cent of turnover; and with some publishers, and in some categories, as high as 70 per cent—astonishing figures indeed and a significant commentary on the world use of the English language and the world respect for English culture. It is one of the pleasanter anomalies of an age of eccentric nationalism that new nations, lacking their own written culture, will adopt an English one: they will prescribe English texts and provide us with the surprising picture of black or yellow infants being examined on the contents of *Our Village* and the *Vicar of Wakefield*. Nor have publishers been backward in establishing indigenous publishing houses in developing areas; perhaps indeed too forward.

Some publishers hold, and the figures seem to support them, that the export trade is growing at the expense of the home market. Useful as exports are they are not always welcomed by publishers, because traditionally high discounts—up to 50 per cent—are expected and given. If a publisher allows 50 per cent and pays his agent 10 per cent of the remainder, there is not a lot left for publisher and author after production costs have been paid. But publishers are unlikely to lose enthusiasm for export markets, since larger editions permit a lower unit price overall, and, in any case, they would sooner sell books than keep them in stock. The combined pressures of economics and a certain patriotic pride, with the willingness of America, and even Russia, to fill any vacuum, will ensure the *status quo*.

Sales to the United States are of two classes. There are 'rights' sales, in which the American publishers produce the book in the States, sometimes photographing the type of the English edition. On these, naturally, a normal royalty is paid. More frequently physical stocks are sold with a cancelled English title-page and a new wrapper. These books are of the specialist kind, costly in production and small in sales, often sold at very high prices in the United States. The only thing to be said in favour of the physical sale is that it clears stocks, pleases authors, and relieves financial anxiety: and that is a lot. But, on such transactions, discounts are high, varying from 60–70 per cent of the United Kingdom price, and the author's royalty is calculated on the price received by the English publisher—rather less than half of that on copies sold in the English market.

A high proportion of English books are 'published' in the United States, one way or another. In addition to regular trade publishers there are in the United States a number of importers-cum-publishers whose business it is to supply institutional libraries with imported books. One or two of these library suppliers are of considerable size and importance, handling a remarkable volume of business. They perhaps exist because the giant-size American publisher, unlike his English equivalent, is interested almost exclusively in books with big selling potential and scoffs at the infinite labour of unloading a small edition of a specialist book.

Unless your publishing concern is a large one, or specializes in best-selling authors' books, there will be little interest in translations into foreign languages. Occasionally the Sales Department will pick up the odd £50, but that is about the extent of it. For the ordinary publisher his physical sales to Germany, France, Switzerland and the Scandinavian countries are far more important.

[5]

The Booksellers

The function of a general bookseller at best is to promote the sale of books; at least to be a channel through which books may be ordered. By ordering his books in advance of publication he receives generally, for his enterprise, a third off the retail price; but he can stock up after publication on the call of a representative at 'journey terms' or by ordering minimum quantities direct. On orders for single copies posted to publishers he receives terms varying from 20 per cent to a third off. This system of calculated incentives may be outdated by the time this book is published, since the protagonists of the 'flat third' and more are fighting vigorously, and in some cases have gained a 35 per cent discount on general books.[1]

A proportion of the turnover of a good bookshop is not the result of having books in stock but lies in his willingness to obtain them. These books are ordered from publishers as required and the process is a laborious, and therefore costly, one. Despite oft-repeated criticism in the press it is a miracle that a book ever passes from producer to buyer. While the book-buyer may be irritated that the book he wants is not in stock, he should recall that at any moment he may walk into a bookshop and order any one of nearly a quarter of a million titles in print. There are

[1] At the Booksellers' Association Conference in 1970 (as reported in the *Bookseller*) the assembled booksellers called for 'at least forty per cent', and, asked Mr Bailey, first vice-president, 'What is going to happen in five or ten years' time, when possibly 40% is not then enough?'

booksellers who will refuse to order books not in stock; they are still in a minority. Many booksellers will not *offer* to do so, for the bookseller must look it up in his trade tools, discover the publisher, write out an order, post it, receive the book and deliver it to his customer, and evolve a system to take care of the operation—which won't leave much change out of a 25 per cent margin, either for publisher or bookseller. It can safely be asserted that this kind of detail is the bugbear of trade profitability. Experiments are being made to cheapen and speed this service by book numbering, but have so far failed to please anyone who prefers and understands Dickens's *David Copperfield* to '212 35969 x'.

Richard Blackwell, of the firm of Basil Blackwell, has printed in *Aslib Proceedings* (Vol. 14, No. 3, 1961) the following details of the life of a bookseller:

'There are some 300,000 different books currently in print in Britain alone. It is impossible to estimate the number of publishers responsible for this output. The Publishers Association alone has some 380 full members. *The Handbook of Publishers and Addresses* contains approximately 1,600 addresses and to these must be added a considerable number of institutions, learned societies, associations, industrial firms, local government offices and even private individuals.

'It is, and must be, the bookseller's function to obtain this enormous variety of items from this great range of sources, keeping in stock as wide a selection as he can. His problem can be contrasted with, for example, the business of Marks and Spencer, which the year before last had a turnover of £148,000,000 (or between three and four times that of the whole home book trade turnover), selling some five hundred articles which, even if allowance is made for all variations in size, colour, and so on, could be estimated not to exceed 5,000 items. The book trade has been compared with the record business, but the record business only has 26,000 records currently in print, and you can see that 26,000 is very different from 300,000.

'This, indeed, is not the full measure of the bookseller's problem. These hundreds of thousands of items are in a constant state of flux. Over 23,000 new titles and new editions are being added each year, and many thousands go out of print at the same time. Many titles, although currently in publishers' lists, go in and out of stock. The book that was available yesterday is binding today and may be available next spring; or a new edition is in preparation and may be available next autumn.

'To illustrate the points I have made I will give you some figures we collected when we recently analysed a day's orders at Blackwell's. We received orders for a total of 3,198 items from forty-three countries. If we exclude orders for periodicals, music, second-hand, American and foreign items we are left with:

2,786 books published by British publishers. Of these we had 1,188 in stock. The remaining 1,598 were ordered from 246 publishers, including 37 who do not appear in the list of publishers and their addresses. 192 items were reported "not yet published". 141 were reported "binding", "reprinting" or "out of stock", and these we recorded and hoped to supply in due course if they became available within a reasonable time, and near the original price. 180 were reported "out of print".'

Here, of course, we are dealing with one of the world's great bookshops, but their difficulties are those of the smaller shop writ large. To reduce this ordered chaos to a functional process, some publishers have pooled their warehousing, dispatch, invoicing and collection of money into the co-operative called Book Centre, with a turnover of some millions of pounds a year, and some 10 per cent of all trade turnover. There are facilities for the centralized payment of booksellers' accounts, for the centralizing of orders and a special service centre for small or single-copy orders. Other publishers co-operate in creating dispatch and travelling arrangements; and some publishers use part of the Book Centre service; and clearly, despite assertions to the contrary, nobody is sitting in the middle of the affair looking complacent. Nevertheless, all these experiments constitute an acceptance by the trade that if books are printed by the thousand they are sold one at a time and that a large part of bookselling is not concerned with selling books to people but particular books to particular people.

Apart from the books he gets 'to order' how does a bookseller set about selling books? He displays his stock and uses his window. He can obtain help from the publishers in the way of display material and lists and prospectuses, and most publishers will give material help in promotion effort. He will look at the important new books shown by travellers and speculate as to who might buy them and to whom he might send a prospectus. From time to time he will either issue his own lists of books recommended, especially at Christmas, the great time of buying, or he will join in and buy a co-operative list paid for in the main by publishers through such an organization as Book Mailing Services. Occasionally he will take a fancy to a particular book and sell many copies on the basis of his own enthusiasm. He will be in touch with the local librarian, and perhaps other 'quantity buyers', to whom he is obliged to give a 10 per cent discount. 'A bookseller is a more important man to the community than a single publisher or even a single author could ever be,' bravely asserted G. R. Davies, when secretary of the Booksellers Association, and evidently the Restrictive Practices Court believed him (and the Publishers Association) for the book trade is one of the few now allowed to operate net prices.

An examination of the orders received in a publisher's office is a more chastening experience. Speaking for myself I can say that nearly 70 per cent of my orders are for single copies of books, many of which have an invoice value of less than a pound. I accept this situation for most of my list, since it could be regarded as being unsuited to the stock of a general bookshop of medium size. But small number of titles are 'bread and butter' books which should be stocked by most bookshops. Single-copy orders for these books are a procession of lost opportunities. What is one to think of world-renowned bookshops which order single copies persistently of a book that sells thousands a year, and has done so for years?

Single-copy trade is, as we say elsewhere, necessary to the book business; there is no escaping it and publishers and booksellers must hope, since it is not profitable in itself, that other parts of their business will stand the strain. But the persistent ordering of bread and butter stock in penny numbers in the hope that publishers will eventually concede larger discounts on such orders is not only a disservice to book-buyers but an unnecessary loss to bookshops. What sales could many books achieve given some encouragement? Some books survive the reluctant bookseller; others, alas, die of sales starvation, for it is almost impossible to get through an edition of, say 3,000 or 5,000 copies of a book at a single-copy pace. This to me is the sad thing about much bookselling: school library orders, public library orders, insistent customer orders, but rarely a copy 'on spec' and for basic stock.

Single-copy orders usually carry a discount less by some 8 per cent than orders for two copies or more. So that whether a bookseller's profit-and-loss account is satisfactory or not must partly depend on the proportion of single-copy orders in his business. We will see that, deplorably, the net return of real bookshops is only 3 per cent of turnover, but I suggest that this is at least in part a self-induced loss and that a clamour for a 40 per cent discount now loudly heard is unrealistic and could result in a substantial increase of book prices, falling largely upon a public unable or unwilling to pay more. Some 70 per cent of a publisher's business is institutional, one kind and another, and institutions do not automatically increase their book-buying allowances year by year, and indeed in some years—as at present—find them reduced. As a result fewer books are bought. In any case the ability of the publisher to provide very high discounts depends upon the popularity of some books and the unpopularity of others. This results in nearly-impossible prices for small editions and easy prices for large editions. An overall high discount would exacerbate a price differential for which the public to whom a book is a book would see no justification.

David Roy, a famous manager (and a bookman) of W. H. Smith's, used to tell me that what worried him was not the books left in his stock but the books not in stock. The opposite view is now too often taken, that a book not bought is a book not left in stock. Stock, say the accountants, must be kept to an absolute minimum and must be turned over X times a year. This is, of course, the 'stores' attitude to goods, that if a square foot of counter space does not earn so much a week then it must be changed for something with a faster turnover. It is but a short step from this attitude to thinking that a good book is a book that sells at once and a bad book one that sells in a day or two. At Smith's the process has now reached alarming lengths. In a recent programme their top man described the firm's plans to limit the promotion of Christmas books to thirty titles and described this as a service to the public.

It is all very well by observation, by computerization, to show that most sales from least effort are concentrated on cheap dictionaries, cookery books, ready reckoners and best-selling merchandise, but this assessment may be underestimating the intelligence and potential of the public, as it must certainly discourage the habitual book-buyers. Since such cynicism must always seek lower and lower levels of literacy, it must meet the fate of Hollywood's film tycoons, who, at the end, found their soufflé unacceptable, and twenty years after a very bad joke. You can only progress downhill in cultural terms by following figures blindly, and perhaps in accountancy terms too, for statistics can never tell you what the public will buy in the way of new ideas put before them. Statistics only show that, given no alternative, the public will buy what is put before them.

Historically the merchandisers, 'there is no difference between soap and books', may be awarded medals for having made retailers look twice at the world in which they find themselves, in changing from a medieval faith in the sanctity of their calling to the brash economics of self-service, undedicated staff, high rents and long leases. Some famous bookselling firms, unable to stand it, have quietly put up their shutters and stolen into oblivion. For others the new climate is wholly acceptable and they see unsuspected beauties in packets of toiletries.

I have laid some stress on the contribution of buying practice to a state of affairs in which the man who sells books and nothing else gets (according to the annual report of the Charter Group of the Booksellers Association) a return on turnover of only 3 per cent and on capital invested 12 per cent. It is pathetic, and a temptation to go into fancy goods on which the return is twice as high; but a happier state of affairs does not necessarily arise from higher discounts but better display, bigger sales, faster turnover, new ideas, just as the sale of cigarettes is profitable on discounts of only 15 per cent. It would be unfair, however, not to mention what seems to be a second handicap to prosperity. While the general publisher tends to give today something near a 30 per cent average discount to bookshops, on school textbooks and technical and scholarly books his discount can amount only to 20 per cent, and where such books are supplied to public libraries a 10 per cent discount is expected and given: this pulls down the bookshop margin considerably. These publishers defend themselves on the grounds that they, and not the bookseller, do the selling, and this is often quite true. But it is, of course, monstrous that a discount to the retailer is on a level at which mere survival is impossible. It is sustained on a basis of blackmail—that a bookseller must get these books if he is to satisfy important customers. Not only does this practice diminish the retailer but forces upon the general publisher the job of subsidizing the educational publisher. General publishers will continue to raise their discounts to bookshops, but specialist publishers must also provide discounts on which bookshop survival is possible.

No doubt all these complaints look very different from the viewpoint of the bookseller and we must feel sympathy for the retailer faced with the problem, physical and financial, of attempting to represent the prolific output of publishing in a 'representative' stock, facing also a population which, because of our educational system, does not attach importance to books as an essential ingredient to full living. Nor must I give the impression that the substance of good bookselling is not to be found in this country. In and out of London there are a hundred bookshops which buy books in a substantial way from the higher levels of publishing: they are to be found in London, in Oxford and Cambridge, in such university towns as Bristol and Edinburgh and in the industrial areas of Manchester, Birmingham, Leeds, Sheffield and Liverpool. Nor must we forget the smaller vocational booksellers in the country and market towns of Britain: in Salisbury, Colchester, in Exeter, in Bath, for that matter in Bournemouth, Brighton and Worthing. They exist quietly, except on market days and Saturdays, as outposts of culture and it is a publishing pleasure to note that the traveller's regular call produces orders of some quality. Blackwell's in co-operation with the Oxford University Press have also now established a group of university bookshops (University Bookshop Organization) in various towns in which most of the virtues of good bookselling survive. W. H. Smith also owns a series of 'quality' bookshops, based on Bowes & Bowes of Cambridge and Truslove and Hanson in London.

I must not encourage the notion that there is nothing

between the bazaar-type bookshop and the pedigree shops of favoured cities. More particularly in the industrial cities—in such places as Blackburn, Newcastle, Northampton, Nottingham, Leicester—there is a type of unpretentious bookshop which caters not only for the confirmed book-buyer of ancient habit but also for the new and inquiring reader, shops which convey the impression that books are both precious and commonplace, things to inspire and tools for living. Such shops are perhaps the most desirable of all in adding enlargement to civilization, and we should pray for their increase, for they neither insult your intelligence nor patronize your taste. In their impression of 'open sesame' they seem to be typified by Foyle's of Charing Cross Road, perhaps the best and biggest booksellers in the world, and certainly, outside W. H. Smith's, the only bookshop known to the common man. At the opposite pole are the admirable Hatchard's where the atmosphere is elegant and the politeness and efficiency extreme: and Dillons—the University of London Bookshop, where books and beards abound.

The booksellers which bring most consistent pleasure to the hearts of publishers are the 'library suppliers', so-called. These firms specialize, as their names suggest, in the sale of books to public and institutional libraries. They have a very particular and enterprising method of working. By call or by correspondence they make the new books known to librarians, first by means of wrappers or announcements, and later through the medium of proofs and finished copies. This sales material is happily supplied by publishers, who are so intoxicated by the sight of enterprise and the large orders that emerge from it that they often give extra discounts. Library suppliers range the country energetically and a local librarian in Dorset or

Surrey is as likely to be ordering his books from Nottingham or Preston as from his home county. They cannot
provide more than the standard 10 per cent discount
permitted by the Net Book Agreement; and, in truth, the
librarian has his own problems in trying to place local
orders, for, as often as not, the only 'bookseller' in his
neighbourhood is a newsagent. My estimate for my own
type of publishing is that 70 per cent of all book sales are
to world-wide institutions: the libraries of schools and
universities, public and county libraries, society libraries,
Government departments and so on.

Such booksellers service the professional, whose
business it is to *find out* which books are published.
For him a remarkably complete record exists. He has
resort to the *Bookseller*, to the *British National Bibliography*, to the Whitaker lists, to the National Book
League's Exhibitions, to the British Council's *British
Book News*; and he refers also to *Trade News* (from W. H.
Smith), especially to a feature written by Whitefriar, the
most gossipy and compulsively readable columnist in the
business, and to *British Books*. With these trade tools, and
with glances at publishers' lists, prospectuses and advertisements, he is fully informed as a person who *wants* to
buy books. If he is a public librarian he will also receive
help from the Library Association, with its several recommending committees and bibliographies.

The public library system has grown quietly but power-
fully. With the inter-lending systems now available it
might, with some truth, be suggested that no one need
ever buy a book. It can be said that the unspoken but
ultimate aim of the public librarian is that no book should
be purchased by the reader; but if it is true that publishers
cannot live off their sales to libraries it can also be said

that no serious publisher can live without the publi
library trade. It is a cliché of authors when speaking of a
expensive and limited-appeal type of book to say tha
'every library will buy a copy'; but it is not so and two o
three hundred copies will satisfy that demand. Neverthe
less the figures are impressive. The latest United King
dom statistics show a home trade turnover in the Trad
of £76,000,000 (1968). Public libraries purchase
£10,750,000 in the same period. Total loans of book
exceeded 20,000,000 at any particular time drawn fron
more than 11,000 service points. These books cost the tax
payer less than a penny a head, and books in stock i
libraries total over a hundred million![2]

Booksellers and publishers must finally approve th
public (and institutional) library. Apart from its com
mercial support libraries are concerned, as are booksellen
and publishers, with the cultural climate of a country an
can no more be regarded as blacklegs than the musi
trade can complain about the playing of Beethoven on th
radio. They are also the main artery of communicatio

[2] 'Saying that the cost of books has continued to rise, "alarmingl
in many cases", the Eastbourne borough librarian Mr A. G. ¦
Enser, in his annual report, tells readers some idea of the value ¦
the books supplied to them. "An estimate of an average family's us
of the home-reading facilities for a year, in the terms of the overa
cost if all the books had been bought by them, is revealing," l
writes. "For example, a family consisting of parents and tw
children, visiting the library once a week and reading two bool
each totals 416 books in a year."
'At an average price of 35s. per book, this represents £72
worth of books entering that household in a year. An annual issue ¦
1,165,000 at 35s. average price of book and 31,000 registere
readers means that each of our readers takes home £700 worth ¦
books a year. Per each inhabitant of the town an average of £3(
worth of books a year are borrowed for a cost to each person ¦
19s. 5d. plus the many additional facilities of the public libra
service.' *The Bookseller*, 3 October 1970.

with the unsophisticated reader. In any case it now seems likely that the book-borrowers may be made to pay something for this privilege under the Public Lending Right proposals of Sir Alan Herbert, the Society of Authors and the Publishers Association.

There was a time, and it lasted until about fifteen years ago, when the commercial lending library could be said to play a significant part in the circulation of books. Several of them had 'preferential' or 'on demand' subscriptions, meaning that a person of selective taste could require the library to obtain any book he wanted within wide limits. Harrod's, The Times Bookshop and, biggest of all, Boots had commercial libraries of value to publishers of serious books, but all have now gone, and there only remain the survivors of 'twopenny' libraries in obscure newsagents' shops.

The multiple or chain store now plays a smaller part in the distribution of books above the level of merchandising than some years ago. Several of these groups, mostly controlled by publicly-owned shares, have gone far in the direction of merchandising in various degrees, though of W. H. Smith it can still be said that books may be ordered through their shops, and this is a considerable service. They will still order quantities of books of some literary or even scholarly merit within their range of subjects; and they must be given credit for trying to withstand the avalanche of pornography which presently menaces the trade.

The New Uses of Literacy

A middle-aged man, casting backwards and forwards, might be forgiven for regarding the future of the Trade with misgiving. It seems a great distance away when John Murray gave his dinners to the assembled booksellers and, having filled them with unaccustomed food and drink, invited them to take up his edition of Livingstone's *Travels*. He is bemused, on television, by the sight of 'publishers' looking like disc jockeys and pop stars calling themselves publishers; he looks uncomprehendingly at interviews with teen-age girls explaining, in lisping accents, how they have spent a few days 'writing' a best-seller, perhaps as far away from real life as the fabrications of Charlotte Young and Mrs Henry Wood. He has seen the Trade, solid, respectable, an occupation for gentlemen, change into a very lively business indeed, and fully in the market place.

Before we consider those aspects of the Trade which are likely to change even more we can look at those which will create a barrier to change; indeed, it is difficult, physically, to see how books, born nearly perfect four hundred years ago, can undergo a sea-change equivalent to that from radio to television or even from acoustic to hi-fi recording.

Fed by weekly lists of best-selling fiction, fashionable history, travel and biography, the average reader of books gets the idea that the world of books is in continuous and rapid flux. The Trade's turnover does not, in the main, come from current best-sellers: they are the jam on the bread. The daily bread is drawn from the stock of a quarter of a million established titles as presented in the heavy weight *British Books in Print*. This sheet-anchor of the Trade—weighing twelve pounds—is composed of lists of books of reference, general books of information, textbooks, classics series, standard fiction, poetry and essays. Many have been long established: a Greek lexicon, like Liddell & Scott, or the *Oxford Concise Dictionary*, might be good for a hundred years.

All publishers hunger for such books, but the going is not so easy as it was. Apart from the inertia that comes of owning a gold-mine, problems of re-presenting and re-styling, perhaps of several scores of titles in a series, creates frightening financial problems. What has been an economic advantage—the ability to produce reprints at small capital cost—could in a period of rapid change become an economic handicap. In such cases there is an obvious parallel with the landlord of an old property: if he has not the resources to rebuild he must content himself with what modernization he can afford. Such a situation helps the new publisher if he can obtain financial backing, since we live not only in a period of technological but cultural change: all history is being assaulted at this moment.

But there is still among publishers the feeling that there is nothing so valuable as a back list well-rooted in *British Books in Print*. New firms have to run hard to stay in the same place and they must try to make profits on current production while the old-timers are taking a leisurely lunch at the Athenaeum. The rub is to find the capital, and this we mention elsewhere. Shortage of financial resource forces the newer publisher into what are called in the Trade 'in and out projects'—you succeed or you fail with a title in a matter of weeks.

The taste of the book-consuming public is also a stabilizing factor. The publicity around some modern novels should not blind us to the fact that many novelists whose books are never reviewed sell large numbers of their books. It would be invidious to name them, but they live comfortably enough in snug houses and gardens in the Home Counties, and the heavy jewellery visible on the breasts of members of the Romantic Novelists' Association looks more reassuring than the hairiness of their contemporaries. In matters of morality, too, there are more Mrs Whitehouses around than the climate-makers of our time would believe. A brief period in a library or bookshop will reveal the massive inertia, the evidence of conservative tastes beneath the shattering impact of contemporary writing. We have elsewhere mentioned the commitment of education syllabuses to ancient texts and old classics, often in specified editions; and this will change but slowly.

But new kinds of presentation as well as new kinds of books will be forced upon our ageing publisher—though with the sure faith that there will always be a field for ever Caxton, the hungry machinery will not be denied. The surge of paperbacks is, in part, a process of new presentation. However expensively, the design and packaging of books must follow the trend elsewhere, from the glossy wrapper inwards.[1] New design, and new market orienta-

---

[1] 'Last year one of the leading record companies attempted to economize on covers. After all they cost 1s. each on an ordinary L.P., and nearer 3s. 6d. each for a prestige album, a sizeable chunk out of the 20s. 3d. that the manufacturers charge the retailer for an L.P. But its competitors persevered with lavish designs, and the company was forced to conform. The trend seems inevitably towards more costly packaging until the day eventually arrives when playable record covers become a technical possibility.'

ion, will be associated with the idea that illustration is of great importance, if only to rival the visual appeal of television. Today it is nearly unthinkable that a book of information should not be illustrated, and often in colour (and there is no cheap way of producing colour). Certainly the younger reader expects its communications to be visual even where visuality is not particularly useful. In such a climate it might be thought that publishers would become film-makers and film-makers publishers; and this is indeed coming about, more so as American publishers invade England. With this swing to illustration we are also seeing a number of outsiders, non-publishers, like the Automobile Association and Reader's Digest, coming into visually-based publishing on the realization that their captive market has an immense book-buying potential in this area. Even the B.B.C. in association with television programmes has immensely widened its book-publishing activities.

If a common factor in all these developments is the impact of illustration, usefully or not usefully, a related assault will follow on the long-cherished idea that what the writer writes is sacrosanct. Publishers' editorial and design departments are beginning to tell authors what should be done not only in the matter of presentation but how the writing and communication should be done. I am here talking of books of fact and justifying aggression on the grounds that if a publisher suggests a subject and outlines its treatment, and is prepared to risk a thousand or two thousand pounds in production costs, he has a right to be in at the end as at the beginning.

A tremendous upsurge of publishing production is under way, but, as we have noted, the recalcitrant problem is distribution; too many books die of neglect; we are in the business of communication but are not communicating. We have seen that direct mail offers are more and more being engaged upon, that various groups with access to the public are by-passing the bookshops, that book clubs are increasing in numbers and methods. While some of these experiments have been surprisingly successful others have failed. In any case they have not really solved the problem of getting good books into large numbers of homes and families; and the volume of business is not significant in the context of the whole of the Trade's turnover, though it may become significant. For a solution of the mushrooming problems of book distribution (and either it will be solved or the publishing side will blow up) we must still look for an expansion of shop outlets.

Despite the fact that the Net Book Agreement was supported by the Restrictive Practices Court it remains restrictive and hampers the exploitation of book markets. Must the bookshops, we are asked, go the way the old sweetshops and the old tobacconists have gone? Neither the sale of sweets or tobacco, despite weighty social taboos, has suffered as the result of the abolition of price maintenance, and their prices go ever higher, but the cold fact is that it is more difficult to obtain a particular book today than it was twenty years ago; and not least because many bookshops while receiving protection have themselves gone over to merchandising and to selling goods other than books; gramophone records are a popular line, and in certain multiple bookshops it is difficult to find books at all, though the word 'Bookshop' appears on their fascias.

It may be folly to pretend that the extension of bookselling to 'other traders' will produce a better service at lower prices to book-buyers, but at least the inquiring public, often frightened at bookshops, will be exposed, must be exposed, to more points of contact with books. At present the frustration of the inquiring book-buyer is real and substantial and every publisher gets letters from members of the public claiming to have asked at half a dozen bookshops for well-known books without satisfaction. The potential 'fringe' public remains unsatisfied, though the appetite is there, except in so far as serious paperbacks reach about 5 per cent of the total market.

Under present conditions there must build up on retail outlets a pressure which will change and enlarge them. We cannot, as a trade, remain dependent upon the hundred or so retail outlets which mark the present limits of good book service. Such bookshops need not worry that their trade will be eroded, for publishers are so heartened by a show of bookshop enterprise, so elated at the thought of representative stock-keeping, that they will fall over backwards to ensure the survival of the so-called 'pedigree' bookshop. There is no need to deny the right of any new sales methods, whether they be 'other trader', book clubs, direct mail; or to frown at the extension of the number of bookshops, once we admit that the Trade cake is not of a fixed size and that a new and apparently competitive sales process or sales area does not of itself reduce everybody else's share: this has been proved time and again by direct mail, by book clubs and paperback sales, notably and recently by the *Reader's Digest/AA Treasures of Britain*, which sold largely by mail but brought a large dividend to bookshops. Publishers and booksellers must cheerfully face the fact that anything that enlarges the market also enlarges appetite. A taste for good books, as I said earlier, is not easily set aside: and the appetite grows by what it feeds on. We are perhaps lucky in the Trade that new and old processes and techniques of publishing and bookselling can subsist side by side. We must have done with the accountants' assumption that the way to growth and importance is minimum stocks at maximum discounts. It is the assumption of stagnation.

Whatever changes in materials and methods we may see the future pattern of the book trade will be settled by the temperaments of the people working in it, and, if there is something to be said for the idea that publishers are the arbiters of culture, since they do the deciding, this may be considered a solemn thought. The observable personnel of publishing houses makes this prospect alarming, although it is difficult in this context to distinguish between genuine alarm and genuine prejudice. My observations of the young men and women in the trade lead me to expect that, to begin with, they will understand money, certainly in a personal sense, since they are receiving in their apprenticeship salaries which the older men receive at the end of their time. Their faces and style are visible on our screens: their smooth and upper-class charm, their air of being literary chaps, of studied untidiness, behind which, one suspects, lies a ruthlessness which might strip you bare. These young men, if we take them as prototypes, are both more sharply intelligent and less scrupulous than their fathers. In reaching for success they are inclined to calculate what the public will like and be prepared to supply it at the acceptable level—which is not to be confused with what the public wants, since it doesn't want anything until it gets it, and then luxury becomes a necessity. The public has lately liked sex in huge doses, with considerable rations of horror and violence. When the public is bored with straight sex, and that moment is now, they will provide it crooked.[2]

These young men will assess to a remarkable degree how best such books can be marketed to a public at last finding some use for its literacy. They will, with a Sunday feature in mind, persuade famous ascetics and hermits to write as if their private lives had been a scandal now made a public one. If they want authors for their kind of book they will somehow get them, not hoping, as in the old days, for a paperback edition, but, working on assurances received, calculate their advances on a scale horrifying to the timid minds of older publishers.[3] They will thrust aside all books without a large sales potential, and they will persuade dons and scholars to write 'explosive' books directing their scholarship to the target of clipping the dignity, not to say the assurance, of human beings; and these same dons, used to obscurity and the sale of hundreds only of their books, will find themselves in the bestseller lists and facing batteries of television cameras.

Much of what has been said in this book reveals the

[2] A recent archetypal blurb: 'Matthews, uneasily wooed and married by his childhood friend Jane, is seduced by Reg, his brother-in-law and one-time lover, into the art forgery business.' Which, like *Lincoln's Doctor's Dog*, has everything. The current best-seller with six-figure sums being aired, is *Everything You Always Wanted to Know About Sex But Were Afraid to Ask*. So far 700,000 copies have been sold in America and it is expected to repeat that success throughout the world.

[3] 'Top publisher of 1970? If there were such an award it would surely go to (naming a well-known younger publisher). Looking through the spring list one repeatedly comes across names that were attached to other houses with their last books. At the present rate of acquisition, there will be just the one major fiction house in about five years' time.' From the official booksellers' journal: *Bookselling News*.

two insistent pressures which must be ameliorated (they cannot be resisted) if the Trade is to perpetuate the values of what we must call, at risk of ridicule, Western civilization. These values are real and have produced many life-enhancing riches. The pressures are inflation and merchandising, different sides of one medal. It does not matter specially if you eat margarine of butter, use brown or black polish, or whether your toothpaste has a minty flavour; but it does matter which books you read. I remarked earlier that forty years ago there was no way of continuing your education without books; they were the only means by which civilization could be carried on. They still remain the best means. They also provide the medium through which the variousness of humanity can be satisfied for every person biologically is an individual, and this is nature's marvel. Merchandising and technology have different ideas; in the interest of convenience it must rob us of our individuality of choice. Fortunately publishers are obstinate people with a firmly-held belief that not all the work of our fathers has gone for nothing; and the Trade remains, as before, a mixture of business and evangelism. The great publishing houses show little inclination to become totally commercialized. Improving books, consistent with human dignity, continue to be published, and, better still, books which neither improve nor denigrate, and merely serve to enlarge mankind's stock of useless knowledge, still find their way into print. If the number of persons living on books as part of the entertainment syndrome has increased, there yet remain enough 'real' books to satisfy all comers.

Appendix I

A SHORT NOTE ON
THE CASH SITUATION

If you have a fancy for seeing a publisher at his most anxious you must meet him when the auditors are 'in'. This is the moment of truth, though sometimes a protracted one, since auditors often take a long time to 'do the accounts'. There is some excuse for this, for the detail is endless; and it was said by an American take-over publisher, unused to Trade practice, that it is easier to build a space craft than to comprehend the accounting details of publishing. The question is, will he, the publisher, be allowed to go on enjoying himself in his agonized way for another year? And be paid for doing it?

When his accountant has sorted things out the publisher must first look at his gross margin, from which his overhead expenses must be deducted to arrive at what are jestingly known as net profits, but from which the tax collector will take half. If his gross margin is less then 40 per cent the publisher must add another crease to his brow, for it is unlikely that his expenses and royalties will be less than that figure.

The percipient reader will note that such a gross margin is much lower than that arrived at in his budgeting (see Appendix II). This is because the publisher has looked at his stocks and, steeling himself to recognize his swans as geese, has decided that many of the books he has recently published are unlikely to sell out their editions and make the profit so confidently set down in theory. So he must write down the remaining stocks below cost, to six months' sales, twelve months' sales, or remainder value. This humbling experience will significantly reduce his margins. In an old publishing house, with a back list of books already prudently written down, this current write-down is well insured from the past; with a new publisher there is no such insurance.

These are the basic elements of publishing accounting. At best (I am not talking about big sellers) a publisher will have to go through three-quarters of his edition to reach profitability; at worst he may decide that he cannot price his book at a ratio of four to one on manufacturing and, unless he pays no royalty, he is lost. In my own firm we make our *budgets* (unless we are deliberately not looking for so high a figure) at a 15 per cent on turn-over (about 10 per cent on retail price) spread over, say, three years; not exorbitant, I think, especially when so-called 'close' companies can be compelled by law to pay 60 per cent of their profits as tax.

After that there is little to say about profit and loss that your accountant won't know about, but a word about money is perhaps justified in a trade as peculiar as publishing. Since sales are slow most of the publisher's capital, in newer houses, tends to be locked up in stock and the amount of capital needed is high in relation to turnover. You will be lucky perhaps to make your real capital turn over three times a year. Thus on £100,000 of turnover you will need about £30,000 in capital, and at £100,000 a year a publishing business is beginning to have substance —this can be regarded as the minimum capital on which to start publishing.[1]

If our serious publisher wishes to grow larger he will

---

[1] I am talking of a 'solid' publishing house. Leonard Woolf's *Downhill All the Way* and *The Journey Not the Arrival Matters* are worth reading on money and size of a publishing business; but he was lucky in his friends.

probably have to seek new sources of capital, and he will soon outgrow the generous credits of suppliers and the indulgence by his banker. It is no good going to merchant banks, since they seek higher profit and larger sales than can usually be managed by publishers, and they are not interested in potentials. Profitability clearly will not help with penal taxation: this source of growth has virtually disappeared. Expansion is too often managed by take-over by American publishers; and then the dangers, near or far, of editorial policy dictated by shareholders may become acute, and publishing rendered tasteless or even obnoxious. Unless our publisher can find a home with a sympathetic and well-established publisher he would be better to try to stay afloat on his own through the gruelling early years. The future of the small publisher, the individual, in publishing is cloudy. He is running against the tide of our time: financiers responsible to shareholders in public companies calling for massive returns in a massive degree; production combines who want long and simple runs; bookselling oulets to whom the man who wants a particular book is a nuisance. This is a matter with social overtones, for it is a question whether the lasting works of scholarship and literature have come, even in the recent past, from large or small publishing houses.

APPENDIX II.

Production budget for a book published in July 1970

MAKE UP text 180 pp., plates 8 pp.
SIZE 8½ × 7⅞ in. trimmed
BLOCKS 48 line, 15 half-tone
PAPER 20 reams Guardbridge Fine Book Wove, 35 × 45 in., 105 lb., 3 reams Mallex Creamy Art, 23 × 36 in., 70 lb.
BINDING Textis cloth, sewn 16s, Newvap, 28 oz boards.
PRICE 63s.
ROYALTY 10%
PRINTING QUANTITY 2500
UNIT COSTS flat sheets 11/7 binding 2/8 bound copies 14/10½
Sales to cover total cost and overheads on U.K. edition (1750) 1422 copies.

	Estimate £	Actual £	s.	d.
BLOCKS				
line	65	45	15	0
tone	35	40	0	0
PRINTING				
composition	670	668	0	0
corrections	50	51	12	0
MACHINING				
text	270	270	15	6
plates	60	58	8	6
PAPER				
text	170	175	0	0
plates	25	29	15	0
CONTINGENCIES	100			
FLAT				

	Estimate £	Actual £	s.	d.
flat sheets	1,445	1,339	6	0
BINDING				
brass	5	4	7	3
bindery work	330	325	6	0
JACKET	75	175	11	6
PRODUCTION COST	1,855	1,844	10	9
Royalty 1750 at 6/3	551			
10% US receipts	94			
TOTAL COST	2,500			
Sales 1750 at 42s	3,675			
Special sales 750 at 25/2½	945			
Total revenue	4,620			
GROSS PROFIT	2,120			
Overheads & publicity (35%)	1,617			
NET PROFIT